HIGHER CIVIL SERVANTS
IN POSTWAR JAPAN

Their Social Origins,
Educational Backgrounds,
and Career Patterns

AKIRA KUBOTA

HIGHER CIVIL SERVANTS IN POSTWAR JAPAN

Their Social Origins,

Educational Backgrounds, and

Career Patterns

PRINCETON, NEW JERSEY

PRINCETON UNIVERSITY PRESS

1969

Publication of this book has been aided by the
Whitney Darrow Publication Reserve Fund
of Princeton University Press

This book has been composed in Times Roman type.

Printed in the United States of America by
Princeton University Press, Princeton, New Jersey

FOREWORD

This is the second of a series of books growing out of the Political Modernization of Japan Project of the University of Michigan's Center for Japanese Studies. The central role of the higher bureaucracy in the process of political development is one major theme of the series as a whole. The first volume—Dr. Robert M. Spaulding, Jr.'s *Imperial Japan's Higher Civil Service Examinations* published by Princeton in 1967—examined the manner in which the merit principle was formally introduced into the system of recruitment for the higher Japanese civil service in the latter part of the nineteenth century and the subsequent growth and change of the system of examinations and personnel administration with which it was associated. The present work carries this theme forward through a systematic study of the social origins, educational backgrounds, and bureaucratic and postretirement careers of a sample of 1,353 individuals who have held the post of section chief or above in the central bureaucracy during the years from 1949 to 1959. A third volume, which is now nearing completion, will perform the same office for a comparable sample of the higher bureaucracy during the 1918-1945 period. Subsequent volumes will treat still other aspects of the political modernization process in Japan.

While all of these volumes relate specifically to the Japanese experience, they have been designed with the hope that they might also be of interest and value as case studies for use by those interested in cross-national comparisons of political systems and patterns of political development. Their authors have taken considerable pains to familiarize themselves with the principal studies of other national bureaucracies, to profit from the experience of such studies and, insofar as possible, to set forth their data and findings in terms that will render them amenable to comparative analysis.

The Political Modernization of Japan Project, of which this volume is a part, was supported by a generous grant from the Carnegie Corporation of New York. We would like to take this opportunity to acknowledge this support and to express our gratitude to the Corporation.

Robert E. Ward

*Director, Center for
Japanese Studies,
University of Michigan*

Acknowledgments

IN writing this monograph I have accumulated a number of debts among faculty members of the University of Michigan. Professor Leslie Kish advised me on the sampling phase, and Professor Warren E. Miller on the analysis phase of this study. Professor Donald E. Stokes, who first exposed me to the quantitative study of politics, also guided me in both of these phases. Dr. Robert M. Spaulding, Jr., participated in other phases including reading earlier drafts of this manuscript, offering comments, and suggesting stylistic changes. Also scholars and specialists in Japan assisted me in carrying out this study. Professor Miyake Tarō of Waseda University and Messrs. Yagura Ichirō and Kanazashi Kin'ichirō of the National Personnel Authority read this manuscript and offered suggestions. I am particularly indebted to Professor Robert E. Ward, chairman of the research project as a part of which this study was undertaken, without whose guidance, assistance, and encouragement this monograph would not have been completed.

The research on which this study is based was made possible by a grant from the Carnegie Corporation of New York to the University of Michigan supporting a series of studies on the political modernization of Japan.

AKIRA KUBOTA

Ann Arbor, Michigan
December 1, 1967

Contents

CONTENTS

Tables

TABLES

TABLES

Figures

FIGURES

HIGHER CIVIL SERVANTS
IN POSTWAR JAPAN

Their Social Origins,
Educational Backgrounds,
and Career Patterns

CHAPTER 1

Introduction

THE political, economic, and social importance of the bureaucracy is manifest today in every nation which has passed beyond the tribal stage of development. In developing nations, the bureaucracy almost always bears major responsibility for whatever is or is not being done for social, economic, and political modernization. In advanced nations, the bureaucracy tends to expand in size, power, and scope of activity, entering increasingly into sectors previously regarded as private. Japan has moved from the first to the second of these stages in the past century, and its bureaucracy has been deeply involved since 1868 in the development of industry, commerce, communications, transportation, education, and agriculture.[1]

In theory, a bureaucracy merely implements policy decisions made by political leaders, but in practice it is hard to distinguish clearly between the making and the carrying out of governmental decisions.[2] Laws and ordinances enacted outside the bureaucracy often originate within it; policies announced by political leaders

[1] The role of government in these processes is examined by William W. Lockwood in *The Economic Development of Japan: Growth and Structural Change, 1868-1938* (Princeton: Princeton University Press, 1954), especially Chapter 8; Thomas C. Smith in *Political Change and Industrial Development in Japan: Government Enterprise 1868-1880* (Stanford, Calif.: Stanford University Press, 1955); and G. C. Allen, *Japan's Economic Recovery* (London: Oxford University Press, 1958).

[2] See Avery Leiserson and Fritz Morstein Marx, "The Formulation of Administrative Policy" in Fritz Morstein Marx, ed., *Elements of Public Administration*, 2d ed. (Englewood Cliffs, N.J.: Prentice-Hall, 1959), pp. 337-351.

have often been proposed or influenced by career subordinates. In any case, statutes and policies often leave essential details to be determined by administrators, and execution often requires interpretations which can result in substantial modification of legislative intent. Finally, the method and vigor of execution can determine the effectiveness of political decisions. For all these reasons, a bureaucracy possesses considerably more power than the term "implementation" implies.

This is particularly true in Japan because the line of demarcation between policy and career officials has long been fixed at a very high level within the government. Many senior positions which in other bureaucracies are filled by political appointees are in Japan usually staffed by career civil servants. Moreover, the power of the Japanese civil service before 1945 was greatly augmented by the weakness and disunity of the political parties, the stringent limitations on parliamentary power, and the absence of constitutional responsibility of the cabinet to the Diet.

Since World War II, many efforts have been made, with varying degrees of success, to alter the balance of power within the Japanese government. The 1947 Constitution designated the Diet as "the highest organ of state power," gave it the authority to choose the Prime Minister, required that at least a majority of the cabinet ministers be members of the Diet, made the cabinet "collectively responsible to the Diet," and greatly strengthened the legislative and budgetary powers of the Diet. These improvements in the position of the elected legislature, together with strong new guarantees of freedom of speech and of other civil rights, fostered the growth and consolidation of political parties to provide the rudiments of genuine parliamentary democracy. Imbalance between the two major parties has not prevented the minority party from inhibiting or modifying many cabinet policies and decisions which previously would not even have required parliamentary consent.

In addition to these fundamental changes in the relative positions and powers of the executive and legislative branches of the government, the Allied Occupation brought about basic changes in the Japanese civil service itself, culminating in a new National Public Service Law (*Kokka Kōmuin Hō*) passed in October 1947 and enacted in July 1948. Career officials as well as political appointees were made subject to "purge" directives that were designed to exclude from office "undesirable persons" who had been exponents of militant nationalism and aggressive foreign policies. The Occupation criticized the career service as excessively dominated by men trained in law and by graduates of Tokyo Imperial University, and called for much greater functional specialization in the education of future civil servants and much less "favoritism" toward graduates of the most eminent preparatory schools and universities. In addition, the Occupation sought to change the underlying philosophy of bureaucratic service by removing the Emperor from the political process and defining bureaucrats not as "the Emperor's aides" but as "servants of the people." Furthermore, when the Occupation ended in April 1952, it left behind a National Personnel Authority supposedly independent of the cabinet and dedicated to the continuous pursuit of these policy objectives.

These attempts at change affected the political process in Japan in varying degrees and in many ways. Some had profound consequences, some had little visible result at all, and some produced effects different from those originally sought. Bureaucratic reform, for example, was obviously impeded by the practical need to use the existing administrative machinery to carry out the broader program of reform sponsored by the Occupation. The redistribution of political power between the executive and legislative branches also did not in practice go as far as the Constitution implied. But it did go far enough to challenge the traditional prestige of the civil service as a career and to make political careers in the Diet more significant than the careers of higher civil servants, who had previously regarded elective office with considerable scorn.

It is the opinion of most observers that the higher civil service remains a powerful political force in Japan.[3] But it is also evident that the postwar higher civil service has been and still is undergoing further transformations. The scope and permanence of the changes already attempted remain uncertain, as do the ultimate objectives and strength of the movement to reverse Occupation policies and restore parts of the old order. These transformations are occurring not in a vacuum but in the midst of significant changes in the pattern of higher education, in political attitudes, in the allocation of political power, and in the social and economic mobility of many segments of the population. It is to be expected, therefore, that the civil service will show characteristics of both continuity and change.

There is no dearth of impressionistic accounts in Japanese of the bureaucracy before and after World War II. Many of these provide useful insights into the characteristics and attitudes of the men who make up the higher civil service and the ways in which they have or have not changed in recent years. The chief limitation inherent in these accounts, however, is the absence of empirical data that would corroborate or disprove their assertions and conclusions, that would show to what degree their claims are substantiated with respect to the higher civil service as a whole or of particular segments of it, or that would permit valid comparison of these findings with past practice in Japan or with the bureaucratic experience of other nations.

It is the purpose of the present study to provide and interpret such data for Japan in terms of a number of variables, ranging

[3] For instance, Kawai Kazuo in *Japan's American Interlude* (Chicago: University of Chicago Press, 1960), p. 116, describes the bureaucracy as by and large the single most powerful political force in Japan today.

from the family and geographic backgrounds of higher civil servants through their educational training and career patterns to their retirement from the service and post-retirement activities. These are not, of course, the only criteria which need to be used in describing, analyzing, and evaluating a bureaucracy. They do provide, however, a significant basis of quantitative and qualitative data upon which useful comparison with other bureaucracies or with the prewar Japanese bureaucracy may rest.

CHAPTER 2

Scope and Method of Study

IN a national study of civil servants, selectivity is essential not only because they are so numerous but also because they are so dissimilar in function. In legal terms, the Japanese civil service covers a wide range of personnel paid from public funds, including cabinet ministers, Diet members, technicians, diplomats, judges, teachers, policemen, mailmen, clerks, and factory workers. A study ignoring functional differences within such an indiscriminate grouping would mean very little; yet one taking them all into account would be prohibitively cumbersome. The present study therefore focuses upon higher administrators in the executive nucleus of the central government. These are senior civil servants charged with planning, supervising, coordinating, and approving the endless series of actions by government workers which collectively constitute the process of public administration. In defining this group, more specific criteria must be introduced.

SELECTION OF ORGANIZATIONS

In deciding whether or not to include a particular official, the first criterion used is the type of government unit to which he is assigned. The study deals with administrators in organizations which are:

1. primarily executive rather than legislative or judicial, and
2. primarily supervisory rather than advisory or operational.

The excluded legislative and judicial units consist of the National Diet, its auxiliary organizations and the courts, quasi-judicial units such as the Fair Trade Commission (*Kōsei Torihiki Iinkai*), the Maritime Accident Inquiry Agency (*Kainan Shimpanjo*), and the Security Exchange Council (*Shōken Torihiki Shingikai*). On the other hand, the study includes the Justice Ministry and the Legislation Bureau (*Hōsei Kyoku*). Although operationally related to the judiciary and the Diet respectively, these units have always functioned primarily as parts of the executive branch of the government.

The excluded advisory organizations are the many committees and councils created, especially after World War II, to study and recommend policies. There are, for instance, several dozen of these attached to the Prime Minister's Office, such as the Science and Technology Council (*Kagaku Gijitsu Kaigi*) and the Council on the Social Security System (*Shakai Hoshōseido Shingikai*). Many others are found in the Finance Ministry, the International Trade and Industry Ministry, and elsewhere.

The excluded operational units are of three principal types. Each cabinet ministry except Foreign Affairs has a galaxy of subordinate branches or field organizations scattered throughout the nation, such as postoffices, tax and customs offices, forest and park services, local public procurators' offices, regional bureaus of maritime transportation, and local branches for the Construction Ministry and the International Trade and Industry Ministry.[1] Next are the public corporations, especially numerous since World War II, such as the Japan National Railways (*Nihon Kokuyū Tetsudō*), the Japan Telegraph and Telephone Public Corporation (*Nihon Denshin Denwa Kōsha*), the Japan Monopoly Corporation (*Nihon Sembai Kōsha*), and a host of financial institutions. Finally, there are state-owned schools, research institutes, observatories, hospitals, factories, and the like. By exception, however, the study does include officials of the Printing Bureau (*Insatsu Kyoku*) and the Mint

---

[1] The Foreign Affairs Ministry did have one Local Liaison Office and two Emigration Assistance Offices as of September 1959; these too are excluded here.

Bureau (*Zōhēi Kyoku*), two operational units which the government continues to classify as integral parts of the Finance Ministry.

The residue can be considered the "core" of the executive branch, concerned with "governing" in the strict and highest sense of the term. It consists primarily of the cabinet ministries (*shō*) and the Prime Minister's Office (*Sōri Fu*).[2] The latter is made up largely of a variety of units which cannot be readily assigned to one ministry or another. In addition to the "core," there are a few organizations which are difficult to characterize except as "peripheral" in one way or another. These are included for the purpose of comparison, but all data pertaining to this "periphery" are kept separate from data on the "core" throughout the present study. The "periphery" consists of the following:

1. The Board of Audit (*Kaikei Kensa In*). This is a body legally independent of the cabinet (the Board of Audit Law, Article 1), that amounts, in theory if not in practice, almost to a separate fourth branch of the government.

2. The National Personnel Authority (*Jinji In*). Unlike the Board of Audit, this agency is technically placed within the cabinet. However, it is guaranteed semi-autonomous status (the National Public Service Law, Articles 8, 9, 13, and 24).

3. The Imperial Household Agency (*Kunai Chō*). The postwar incorporation of this unit into the cabinet structure made it theoretically an executive agency. But in reality it has less executive character than before, since the 1947 Constitution greatly curtailed imperial authority in government.

4. Embassies (*Taishi kan*) and Legations (*Kōshi kan*). These overseas offices of the Foreign Affairs Ministry represent the Japanese government in foreign nations. Their functions are unlike those of normal public administration, and their senior personnel

[2] Major units of other types are the Economic Stabilization Board (June 1949–July 1952) and the Attorney General's Office (February 1948–July 1952).

10

are exempted from application of the National Public Service Law (Article 2, par. 11).

Figure 1 shows the organization of the Japanese government in 1959, specifying the "core" and the "periphery," as defined in this study, of the Japanese bureaucracy.

SELECTION OF POSITIONS

The second criterion in selection is the position to which an administrator is assigned within his organization. This is considered in terms of position level, function, and type of appointment. The four basic supervisory position levels recognized by the National Government Organization Law are here referred to as Levels I, II, III, and IV. Functionally, positions are considered on the basis of the degree of specialization. Where type of appointment is concerned, a distinction is made between political (or policy) and nonpolitical (or career) appointments.

It should be noted that in spite of the rapid growth of the Japanese bureaucracy, the internal structure of the ministries is similar. What has been defined as the "core" of the bureaucracy consists of about a dozen (eleven in 1959) ministries plus the Prime Minister's Office. Each ministry is headed by a cabinet minister (*daijin*), assisted by one or two parliamentary vice-ministers (*seimu jikan*). All of these are by law required to resign when the cabinet falls.[3] These are political, not career posts (although they are sometimes filled by former career men), and are therefore excluded from the study.

The highest administrative career position level in a ministry, here termed Level I, is that of administrative vice-minister (*jimu jikan*), and this is the point at which the hierarchy of career civil servants considered in this study begins. Each ministry also has one

[3] The Constitution, Article 66, par. 3; and the National Government Organization Law, Article 17, par. 6.

11

FIGURE 1: THE ORGANIZATION OF THE JAPANESE GOVERNMENT AND
UNITS SELECTED FOR STUDY (SEPTEMBER 1959)

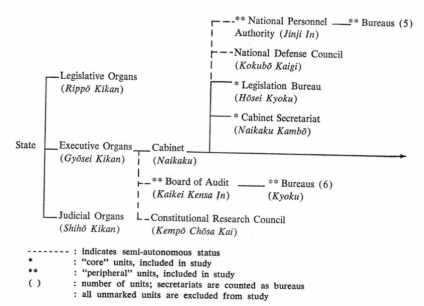

-------- : indicates semi-autonomous status
*   : "core" units, included in study
**   : "peripheral" units, included in study
( )   : number of units; secretariats are counted as bureaus
         : all unmarked units are excluded from study

SOURCE: *Shokuin roku*, 1960 ed., Vol. 1, pp. 1-63.

* Prime Minister's Office ——————— ┌─ * Bureaus (3)
(*Sōri Fu*)   ├─ ** Imperial Household Agency
                                  │   (*Kunai Chō*)
                                  └─ * Other agencies (9)

_ * Justice Ministry —————————— ┌─ * Bureaus (7)
(*Hōmu Shō*)   └─ * Agencies (2)

                                 ┌─ * Bureaus (8)
_ * Foreign Affairs Ministry ———— ├─ ** Embassies (51) and ** Legations (26)
(*Gaimu Shō*)   │   (*Taishi kan* and *Kōshi kan*)

_ * Finance Ministry —————————— ┌─ * Bureaus (8)
(*Ōkura Shō*)   └─ * Agency (1)

_ *Education Ministry—————————— * Bureaus (6)
(*Mombu Shō*)

_ * Welfare Ministry ——————————— * Bureaus (9)
(*Kōsei Shō*)

                                 ┌─ * Bureaus (5)
_ * Ministry of Agriculture and —— └─ * Agencies (3)
Forestry (*Nōrin Shō*)

_ * Ministry of International Trade ┌─ * Bureaus (9)
and Industry   └─ * Agencies (3)
(*Tsūshō Sangyō Shō*)

_ * Transportation Ministry———— ┌─ * Bureaus (8)
(*Unyu Shō*)   └─ * Agency (1)

_ * Postal Services Ministry————— * Bureaus (6)
(*Yūsei Shō*)

_ * Labor Ministry——————————— * Bureaus (4)
(*Rōdō Shō*)

_ * Construction Ministry,————— * Bureaus (5)
(*Kensetsu Shō*)

13

secretariat (*kambō*) and several bureaus (*kyoku*). The secretariat is headed by a chief of secretariat (*kambō chō*), and the bureaus by chiefs of bureau (*kyoku chō*), sometimes aided by one or two assistant chiefs of bureau (*kyoku ji-chō*). These positions are included in the study as Level II posts.

Some secretariats and some—but by no means all—bureaus are organized into divisions (*bu*). Each of these is headed by a chief of division (*bu chō*), who is in a very few instances assisted by an assistant chief of division (*bu ji-chō*). For our purposes these positions are classified as Level III posts and included in the study. The next echelon consists of sections (*ka*), which are responsible either to chiefs of division or, in bureaus not organized into divisions, directly to chiefs of bureau. Each section is headed by a chief of section (*ka chō*), and these positions are included in the study as Level IV posts.

In general, the four levels represent a clear stratification of authority, and Levels I, II, and IV are more or less comparable and are basic units throughout the government. Level III, however, has certain peculiarities in the organization of the Japanese bureaucracy. Divisions are a relatively new intermediate echelon and are found only in limited parts of the government. They tend to be specialized in function, and to vary a great deal in importance. Some chiefs of division have status and powers as great as those of chiefs of bureau, whereas other chiefs of division merely assist chiefs of bureau. Also chiefs of both division and bureau are classified in the same pay category (*tōkyū*).[4] Nonetheless, the two categories are sufficiently different to make useful their classification as separate levels in the study.

In addition to this principal hierarchy of ministry, bureau, division, and section headed by senior career officials at Levels I, II, III, and IV respectively, a number of other units are encountered

[4] The National Personnel Authority Rule, Article 9-8, Attached Table No. 1.

14

within the "core" of the executive branch. These are known generically as external bureaus (*gai kyoku*) but now usually bear the official title of agency (*chō*). Agencies are unevenly distributed among the ministries, while the Prime Minister's Office consists largely of a grouping of heterogeneous agencies.

Each agency is headed by a director (*chōkan*), whose rank and type of appointment vary with the size and importance of the agency. A few agencies, mostly in the Prime Minister's Office, resemble ministries. Their directors hold the concurrent title of minister without portfolio (*kokumu daijin*) and are assisted by parliamentary and administrative vice-ministers. All of these, except the administrative vice-minister, are political appointees, and our selection therefore begins at the administrative vice-minister level, as in the ministries. In other agencies, the director is a nonpolitical appointee and is sometimes assisted by a vice-director (*ji-chō*), also a career man. These are classified as Level I posts because they possess certain powers not granted to Level II officials—notably a limited authority to issue directives.[5]

Agencies may be subdivided into bureaus, divisions, and sections. The heads of these units have the same titles as elsewhere, and for our purposes, are classified in Levels II, III, and IV respectively. In practice, however, few agencies have both bureaus and divisions. In 1949, the highest sub-units tended to be divisions rather than bureaus, but by 1959 divisions had been largely replaced by bureaus, directly subdivided into sections.

Positions in the "periphery" of the bureaucracy are selected and classified in substantially the same way as in the "core." Here again the internal structure is quite uniform. The Board of Audit, the National Personnel Authority, and the Imperial Household Agency may be equated with the agencies (*chō*) just described. For embassies and legations, however, only chiefs of mission, namely ambassadors (*taishi*) and ministers (*kōshi*), are included in this

[5] The National Government Organization Law, Article 13.

15

study. These positions are treated as an independent category distinct from the four levels.

In addition to those who are heads or assistant heads of ministries, bureaus, divisions, and sections, there are a very few higher officials who are not heads or assistant heads of these or comparable units. A few of them are charged with administrative supervision of organizations which are separate from the organizations to which they are assigned. However, a majority are what may be called specialists and are not charged with any administrative responsibility. Now we turn to our final criterion of selection, the function of the civil service position.

In his study of American federal civil service Reinhard Bendix classified civil servants into two groups: those whose task is one of general direction and those whose task is one requiring a specialist's competence.[6] In this study, the same method is used. Those who are heads or assistant heads of ministries, bureaus, divisions, and sections generally perform the former function and are included in our selection. Those who are not heads or assistant heads of these units but are charged with administrative supervision similarly perform the function of general direction and are included in our selection and classified into Levels I, II, III, and IV, depending upon their salaries.[7]

There are a number of higher officials in the Japanese government who generally perform functions requiring a specialist's competence. Their positions clearly demand the skills of scientists, medical doctors, engineers, military officers, lawyers, or other professional persons. However, most of these are located outside the "core" and "peripheral" units of the bureaucracy and are thus already eliminated in the initial selection of units. Specialists found

[6] Reinhard Bendix, *Higher Civil Servants in American Society* (Boulder, Colo.: University of Colorado Press, 1949), p. 15.

[7] See, for instance, the Salaries of General Service Law, and the National Personnel Authority Rule, Article 9-8.

16

in the "core" (in rank comparable to Level IV or higher) but excluded from the study include public procurators (*kenji*) in the Supreme Procurator's Agency (*Saikō Kensatsu Chō*) and education inspectors (*shigakukan*) in the Education Ministry. Advisers (*komon*) and consultants (*san'yo*) to various ministries are also omitted, since they are expected to have highly specialized experience and training, and are usually employed on a part-time basis. Clearly all these positions, unlike those included in the study at Levels I, II, III, and IV, are not primarily concerned with administrative supervision. An exception has been made, however, for a group of councillors (*shingikan*) in the Economic Planning Agency (*Keizai Kikaku Chō*) of the Prime Minister's Office, who are included at Level II. Unlike other advisory positions, these are mostly filled by full-time, nonspecialist career civil servants in the midst of their careers.

Selection of Individuals

The administrative positions selected for study lack fixed terms of office, and changes in personnel occur constantly and irregularly. This presents a problem in determining the point or span of time during the postwar period to which a survey should relate. Between the extremes of examining incumbents in office as of one particular date alone or of examining all who have held these positions during the postwar period, it seemed preferable to study incumbents at several regular intervals during the postwar period.

The starting date, late 1949, was selected for two reasons. By this time, the initial or reform phase of the Allied Occupation had ended, and a greater degree of decision-making authority was being returned to Japan, although complete autonomy was not restored until April 1952. The bureaucracy was again beginning to function as a section of an increasingly independent Japanese government rather than an appendage of the Occupation. Moreover, on

17

June 1, 1949, the cabinet carried out the first wholesale reorganization of the bureaucracy since World War II. The other two years under examination, 1954 and 1959, were spaced at five-year intervals thereafter. Since many of those covered in the study remained in the same position for three or four years, most higher administrators holding office from 1949 to 1959 are covered by this method of selection.

Within the survey years, the incumbents considered are those listed in the annual *Shokuin roku* or register of officials. The specific dates of the *Shokuin roku* for the selected year are September 10, 1949; November 15, 1954; and September 15, 1959. All incumbents in Level I, II and III positions (as defined above) were included in the study. From the far more populous Level IV positions, a random sample amounting to approximately 11 percent was considered for each year.[8] In order to reduce the standard error, each sample was made reasonably large, and was stratified by ministry and drawn in proportion to size.

Table 1 shows the composition and the number of positions in Levels I, II, III, and IV in the "core" of the bureaucracy in 1959. These four levels consist primarily of positions of heads or assistant heads of ministries, bureaus, divisions, and sections respectively, but they also include as indicated in the table those positions which are not heads or assistant heads of these units.

Tables 2, 3, and 4 give a breakdown by year and position level of all the positions—1,353 cases—selected for this study. Table 2 refers to those in the "core," and Tables 3 and 4 to those in the "periphery" of the bureaucracy. There were no ambassadors or ministers for 1949, since Japan did not resume formal diplomatic relations until 1952.

[8] The method of random selection is described in numerous statistical handbooks, e.g., Hubert M. Blalock, *Social Statistics* (New York: McGraw-Hill, 1960), pp. 392-397.

TABLE 1: POSITION AND NUMBER OF HIGHER
CIVIL SERVANTS IN THE CORE (1959)

Level	Positions Included	Number	Total
I	administrative vice-ministers (*jimu jikan*)	12	
	directors (*chōkan*) and vice-directors (*ji-chō*) of agencies (*chō*)	28	
			40
II	chiefs of secretariat (*kambō chō*)	12	
	chiefs of bureau (*kyoku chō*)	106	
	assistant chiefs of bureau (*kyoku ji-chō*) and others of comparable rank.	37	
			155
III	chiefs of division (*bu chō*)	84	
	assistant chiefs of division (*bu ji-chō*) and others of comparable rank.	5	
			89
IV	chiefs of section (*ka chō*)	812	
			812
Grand Total			1,096

SOURCE: *Shokuin roku*, 1960 ed.

TABLE 2: NUMBER OF CORE OFFICIALS SELECTED FOR STUDY,
BY YEAR AND LEVEL

Year	Level				Total
	I	II	III	IV*	
1949	46	117	122	110	395
1954	39	120	92	96	347
1959	40	155	89	90	374
Total	125	392	303	296	1,116

* The populations for Level IV were 970 in 1949, 867 in 1954, and 812 in 1959. For the other levels, the total populations were studied.

SOURCES AND TABULATION

In addition to the *Shokuin roku*, which identifies individual office holders, principal sources for the data presented in the following chapters are dictionaries of contemporary biography. In order

TABLE 3: NUMBER OF PERIPHERAL OFFICIALS (EXCLUDING DIPLOMATS) SELECTED FOR STUDY, BY YEAR AND LEVEL

Year	Level				Total
	I	II	III	IV*	
1949	8	20	3	15	46
1954	8	17	2	15	42
1959	8	20	2	15	45
Total	24	57	7	45	133

* The populations for Level IV were 66 in 1949, 61 in 1954, and 60 in 1959. For the other levels, the total populations were studied.

TABLE 4: NUMBER OF DIPLOMATS SELECTED FOR STUDY, BY YEAR*

Year	Ambassadors	Ministers	Total
1949	0	0	0
1954	21	15	36
1959	53	15	68
Total	74	30	104

* The total population of diplomats of appropriate rank was studied without classification by position level.

to obtain information as comprehensive as possible on date and place of birth, family, marriage, education and careers, several such dictionaries published at different times were used. The most comprehensive series is *Jinji kōshin roku*, which lists virtually all those at Level III and above and most of those at Level IV. The study is based largely on the 1951, 1956, 1961, and 1964 editions of *Jinji kōshin roku* although other editions were consulted where necessary. Omissions in this series were filled, whenever possible, from other biographical sources, chiefly *Nihon kankai meikan* (1962 ed.) and *Zen Nihon shinshi roku* (1961 and 1963 eds.). A third major category of sources includes alumni directories of major universities and higher schools. From these varied sources it has been possible to obtain complete or partial data on 97.7 percent of the selected "core" officials and 99.6 percent of the selected "peripheral" officials.[9] (A complete list of sources is given in the Bibliography.)

In the following pages and tables, data collected for the "core" and the "periphery" were always processed and presented separately. For the "core," data are tabulated and analyzed primarily in terms of three variables: (1) position level, (2) ministry, and (3) survey year. All tables and figures include data for Levels I, II, and III, but in some tables, Level IV officials are omitted for various reasons. It is, for instance, almost meaningless to estimate the average retirement age for Level IV, since many of the incumbents at this level did not leave the service during the period of this study. In the tables comparing ministries rather than levels, Level IV is also omitted. The large number of cases in this level would reduce these comparisons to virtually ministerial comparisons of Level IV officials alone, if Level IV figures were added to those for the higher levels and weighted by the inverse proportions of the sampling rates.[10] There were, for example, 35 officials in Level IV in the Construction Ministry in 1949, but the combined total for Levels I, II, and III was only 8; there were 147 Level IV officials but only 37 Level I, II, and III officials in the International Trade and Industry Ministry in the same year. In each table, the coverage in terms of position level or number of cases is specified.

Of the three variables, position level is most susceptible to the analysis of statistical association, and is often used in tables in Chapters 3 through 6. Since this analysis includes some technical problems, a brief explanation is in order. The degree of associa-

[9] Although these sources listed nearly every official studied, they did not necessarily provide data on all the items studied, as shown in varying numbers of cases in tables in this study.

[10] Although the decision of whether or not ministerial comparison includes Level IV officials leads to major differences in interpreting tabulation results, in most cases actual results by the two methods varied only slightly. This was, as will be shown later, due to the high homogeneity of Japanese higher civil servants.

21

tion among variables can be precisely expressed by such indicators as r, τ_a, τ_b, γ, and r_s, but the underlying notion of correlation may be explained without resorting to such technical terms. Table 5 illustrates three major types of distributions so as to assist in understanding degrees of association in tables presented later. It should be noted, however, that the measuring of association in positional data is different from that in other data. A chief difference is that the proportion for the lowest ranking group cannot be expected to be 0 percent.

TABLE 5: THREE HYPOTHETICAL DISTRIBUTIONS OF DATA
ILLUSTRATING DEGREES OF ASSOCIATION

| Variable | *Level* | | | | |
	I	*II*	*III*	*IV*	
A	100%	75%	50%	25%*	Strong Correlation
B	60%	50%	40%	30%	Moderate Correlation
C	40%	40%	40%	40%**	No Correlation (or Independence)

* Distributions of data for promotion differ in at least one respect from other types of data. The proportion for the lowest level cannot be expected to be 0% even in the situation of maximum correlation. There must be some individuals at the lowest level possessing the same feature as those in the highest, if they climb up the ladder and eventually dominate the highest level.

** The specific figure does not have to be 40%. It can be 80%, 50%, 30% or any other, as long as the same value prevails throughout the table.

Reference has already been made to certain similarities between Level II and Level III positions, which might be thought to warrant a combination of these two levels. However, as will be shown below, those at Levels II and III show similar characteristics for some variables but not for others. For this reason, and because of the substantial number of Level III positions, the two have been kept separate, so that points of difference as well as similarity could be clearly shown.

In the "core," averages (or means in statistical terminology) for all administrators are computed on the basis of individual officials. In other words, these averages are weighted by the number of persons adjusted by the inverse proportions of the sampling rates.[11] Some differences in the sampling rates, i.e., 0.11340 for 1949, 0.11073 for 1954, and 0.11084 for 1959 for the "core," and other rates for the "periphery," are also adjusted in this process. Averages based on position levels rather than individual officials can be obtained by summing average values for all levels, as presented in the following chapters, and dividing by the number of levels. As for the "periphery," no overall averages are calculated, since the heterogeneous character of this composite group makes averaging irrelevant for analytical purposes. Finally, when the same individual, holding the same or a different position, appeared in different survey years, he was counted as often as he appeared. The extent of overlapping of individuals is presented in Figure 10 in Chapter 6.

TERMINOLOGY

The "core" and the "periphery" of the Japanese bureaucracy selected for this study include eighteen organizational units of which only twelve are legally called ministries. However, in the following chapters all the eighteen units are often simply referred to as the "ministries" rather than as the "ministries and other organizational units" or any other form of designation especially when data are analyzed on the basis of the organizational structure of the Japanese bureaucracy.

Technically, however, the "core" includes:

1. The Prime Minister's Office*

---

[11] Exceptions are Tables 6 and 7. Weighting is avoided because the numbers of persons should not be, in these cases, expressed in fractions, and because these tables are made largely for illustrative purposes.

* Including the Legislation Bureau and the Cabinet Secretariat. In 1949, the former belonged to the Attorney General's Office.

2. The Justice Ministry**
3. The Foreign Affairs Ministry
4. The Finance Ministry
5. The Education Ministry
6. The Welfare Ministry
7. The Agriculture and Forestry Ministry
8. The International Trade and Industry Ministry
9. The Transportation Ministry
10. The Postal Services Ministry
11. The Labor Ministry
12. The Construction Ministry
13. The Telecommunications Ministry (1949 only)
14. The Economic Stabilization Board (1949 only)

The "periphery" includes:

1. The Board of Audit
2. The National Personnel Authority
3. The Imperial Household Agency
4. Embassies and Legations

For simplicity, the terms "higher civil servants" and "higher administrators" have been used throughout the study generically and interchangeably to mean all the personnel considered here, whether from core or from periphery. However, it should be understood that, as a legal term, "higher civil servants" or *kōtō bunkan* was used before 1948 to mean a much larger group of civil servants, including many below Level IV and many of higher rank who would be excluded from this study for reasons explained above. Use of this term was discontinued in 1948, and the new term *kokka kōmuin* (national public servants) has an even broader meaning. In position level and importance, the personnel con-

** The Justice Ministry was called the Attorney General's office (*Hōmu Fu*) from February 1948 to July 1952.

sidered in this study constitute a bureaucratic elite within the *kōtō bunkan* or *kokka kōmuin*. The comparative size of these two groups and the group here designated as "higher civil servants" or "higher administrators" can be seen from Figures 2 and 3.

FIGURE 2: EMPLOYEES OF THE NATIONAL GOVERNMENT (1959)
(Total: 1,665,761)

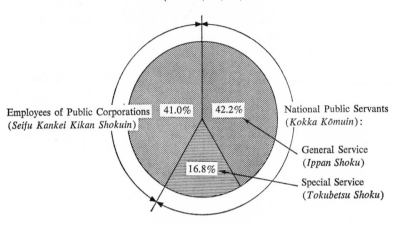

National Public Servants	59.0%	General Service	42.2%					
		Special Service	16.8%	Executive Branch	15.3%	Defence	15.3%	
						Others	0.02%	
				Legislative Branch	0.2%			
				Judicial Branch	1.3%			
Employees of Public Corporations	41.0%							
Employees of the National Government	100.0%							

SOURCE: *Gyōsei kanri nempō*, Vol. 9 (1961), p. 245.

FIGURE 3: NATIONAL PUBLIC SERVANTS, KŌTŌ BUNKAN, AND HIGHER
CIVIL SERVANTS SELECTED FOR STUDY

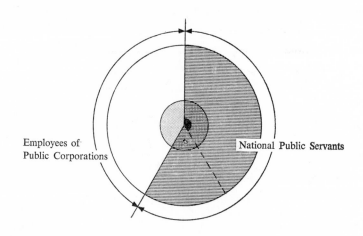

		Number	Proportion
	: Higher Civil Servants Selected for this study (Core and Periphery)	487 in 1959	0.05%
	: *Kōtō Bunkan* (Including *chokunin* and *sōnin*; the group is imposed upon the diagram as if the system had existed in 1959)	54,127 in 1947	5.5%
	: National Public Servants	983,718 in 1959	100.0%

SOURCES: *Japan Statistical Yearbook*, Vol. 3 (1951), p. 350; *Gyōsei kanri nempō*, **Vol.**
9 (1961), p. 245.

CHAPTER 3

Social Origins

PREFECTURAL ORIGINS

THE governments of traditional Japan, being neither federal nor representative, had no attachment to the idea of equal or proportionate recruitment of officials from various regions of the nation. Access to office was based almost always on family or feudal status, and recruitment showed a high degree of geographic concentration. The areas of concentration varied from one period to another, as power shifted from one group to another. Under the Tokugawa feudal rule, for example, central government officials were primarily drawn from territories under the control of the shogun, his relatives, and his close vassals.

After the Meiji Restoration of 1868, the domains which led the anti-Tokugawa movement claimed the lion's share of offices in the new government. In 1874, some 65 percent of all *chokunin* ("imperially appointed") officials and 37 percent of all *sōnin* ("imperially approved") officials came from the four southwestern domains of Satsuma, Chōshū, Tosa, and Hizen.[1] Between 1884 and 1899, however, the government gradually shifted to a recruitment policy based upon competitive examinations. The cumulative effects of this change have brought about, as will be discussed presently, a rather remarkable dispersion in the geographic origins of modern higher officials.

Published biographical sources record either the place of birth or the prefecture of registration for nearly all of those included

[1] Yoshimura Tadashi, *Gendai seiji ni okeru kanryō no chi-i* (Tokyo: Maeno Shoten, 1950), pp. 219-220.

27

in the study. In the following analysis, the place of registration is used when the place of birth is not recorded. These two are, of course, not always identical. There has been a tendency to retain the "original registration" (*honseki*) in the traditional family seat, though the family may have moved long before the birth of the individual in question. Since the general trend of population movement in modern Japan has been from the countryside to urban areas, classification by the place of registration is likely to overestimate the proportion of rural origin. Yet the place of registration does indicate the origin of the present or preceding generation, and it is a place where significant family and other relations exist.

Table 6 presents the prefectural distribution of the 1949-1959 higher civil servants by ministry. It is apparent that recruitment is widely scattered. A broad geographic basis of origin is seen for the bureaucracy as a whole as well as for the individual ministries. The former predominance of men from the four southwestern domains has vanished. In total, they account for barely 8 percent of all the core officials studied (88 out of 1,083). Prefectural distributions controlled by position level or survey year, though not reported here, show a similar pattern of dispersal.[2] It is noteworthy that the distribution is equally widespread among peripheral officials. Those in the Imperial Household Agency and the diplomatic corps, often thought to be recruited from a narrow base, originated in fact from all parts of Japan.

[2] "Control" in statistics generally means methods to remove from the main relationship the influence of those variables which are, for one reason or another, considered to be of secondary theoretical interest in research. (It occurs in such contexts as controlled samples, control groups, a partial regression controlled by the variable A, and a tabulation controlled by the variable B.) Consequently control often sheds additional light upon the pattern of association among those variables which are of primary theoretical interest. When a certain method of control greatly reduces the variance, it may be said that the control variable is strongly related to the main relationship. When it does not, it may be said that the control variable is almost unrelated to the main relationship.

TABLE 6: BIRTHPLACE OF HIGHER CIVIL SERVANTS: PREFECTURAL AND REGIONAL DISTRIBUTION, BY MINISTRY

PREFECTURE	PERIPHERY				TOTAL (CORE only)	CORE													
	Ambassadors & Ministers	Imperial Household Agency	Board of Audit	National Personnel Authority		Economic Stabilization Board	Telecommunications	Construction	Labor	Postal Services	Transportation	International Trade & Industry	Agriculture & Forestry	Welfare	Education	Finance	Foreign Affairs	Justice	Prime Minister's Office
HOKKAIDŌ	2	3	1	1	8	—	1	3	1	—	—	—	—	—	2	—	1	—	—
TŌHOKU:																			
Akita	—	—	—	—	8	—	—	—	1	—	—	—	—	—	—	—	—	3	4
Aomori	1	—	—	2	2	—	—	—	—	1	—	—	—	—	—	1	—	—	—
Fukushima	—	1	—	2	24	2	—	2	5	—	1	—	7	1	—	2	1	1	2
Iwate	1	—	—	—	12	2	1	—	—	—	1	1	3	2	—	—	1	1	1
Miyagi	3	—	—	—	22	—	—	—	—	2	1	3	3	—	—	3	1	1	7
Yamagata	1	4	—	1	11	1	—	—	—	—	—	1	4	1	—	1	1	—	2
KANTŌ:																			
Chiba	4	1	1	2	19	1	—	1	1	—	2	4	1	1	1	—	1	2	4
Gumma	—	—	2	3	14	1	1	—	1	1	3	—	1	—	—	—	—	4	2
Ibaragi	6	—	1	—	25	—	—	2	3	2	2	3	2	1	—	2	2	1	5
Kanagawa	2	—	1	1	24	—	1	—	—	1	1	7	—	2	1	3	—	2	6
Saitama	—	1	—	—	12	—	1	—	2	2	—	1	1	2	—	1	—	1	1
Tochigi	2	—	—	—	5	—	—	—	—	—	1	2	—	—	—	1	1	—	—
Tokyo	27	11	6	10	197	7	5	8	2	12	9	26	20	13	11	25	15	7	37

		PERIPHERY					CORE													
		Ambassadors & Ministers	Imperial Household Agency	Board of Audit	National Personnel Authority	TOTAL (CORE only)	Economic Stabilization Board	Telecommunications	Construction	Labor	Postal Services	Transportation	International Trade & Industry	Agriculture & Forestry	Welfare	Education	Finance	Foreign Affairs	Justice	Prime Minister's Office
CHŪBU:																				
Aichi		3	1	1	—	20	—	1	—	1	—	2	2	3	1	2	2	1	1	4
Fukui		—	2	—	—	12	1	—	—	—	—	—	1	3	1	—	3	—	1	2
Gifu		2	—	—	—	19	1	—	1	—	2	2	2	3	1	—	2	—	2	3
Ishikawa		—	2	2	—	6	—	—	1	—	1	—	2	—	1	—	1	—	—	—
Nagano		2	—	2	1	22	1	2	—	1	1	3	1	—	2	1	—	—	6	4
Niigata		2	1	3	2	27	—	—	—	1	2	3	2	2	5	—	2	3	3	4
Shizuoka		—	—	2	1	29	3	3	2	—	1	1	5	2	—	—	4	—	3	8
Toyama		—	1	—	—	19	—	—	2	—	—	2	—	3	1	—	—	1	1	6
Yamanashi		—	1	—	—	19	1	—	1	—	2	5	1	5	1	—	1	—	—	2
KINKI:																				
Hyōgo		3	—	1	3	53	2	1	—	1	1	8	4	6	3	3	5	3	5	11
Kyōto		4	4	—	—	19	—	1	—	1	2	2	3	2	1	—	1	2	—	4
Mie		—	—	—	—	27	1	1	2	—	3	3	3	1	—	1	1	—	2	9
Nara		2	—	—	—	10	—	1	—	—	—	2	—	1	1	—	—	1	—	5
Ōsaka		2	—	—	1	46	1	—	2	3	2	7	10	4	—	—	5	—	3	8
Shiga		—	—	—	—	6	1	—	—	1	—	—	2	—	1	—	1	1	—	1
Wakayama		5	—	—	1	19	—	—	—	—	1	2	4	2	1	1	3	1	2	2

	CORE															PERIPHERY			
CHŪGOKU:																			
Hiroshima	11	2	—	3	1	7	2	7	2	7	2	—	2	1	48	2	6	1	4
Okayama	5	2	1	5	1	2	1	5	5	3	5	1	1	1	34	5	—	—	1
Shimane	3	1	—	—	—	1	2	3	2	2	—	—	—	1	15	1	—	—	4
Tottori	—	1	1	—	—	3	3	2	1	3	2	2	1	1	16	1	—	—	3
Yamaguchi	5	8	2	3	—	2	4	6	1	1	—	1	2	1	35	—	3	2	2
SHIKOKU:																			
Ehime	6	1	—	1	1	1	6	2	1	3	—	2	—	1	25	2	1	—	2
Kagawa	3	—	—	1	1	1	—	2	1	—	—	1	—	—	9	2	2	—	1
Kōchi	2	—	—	4	—	—	2	3	—	—	—	—	—	—	11	—	—	—	2
Tokushima	2	2	—	—	—	—	1	—	1	1	—	—	—	—	7	—	1	—	1
KYŪSHŪ:																			
Fukuoka	6	1	1	8	1	—	8	9	4	4	2	4	3	3	59	—	1	—	2
Kagoshima	4	—	1	2	1	1	2	8	1	1	2	—	—	—	21	1	—	—	3
Kumamoto	2	1	2	—	2	2	—	2	2	2	2	—	1	2	18	2	1	1	2
Miyazaki	4	1	—	2	—	1	2	—	—	—	—	—	—	1	5	1	2	—	—
Nagasaki	1	1	—	1	—	—	2	—	1	1	—	—	—	—	9	—	—	—	2
Ōita	5	—	—	1	—	—	3	3	2	2	1	1	1	—	14	—	5	—	1
Saga	8	2	2	1	—	—	3	3	1	1	1	1	1	—	21	1	—	—	2
SUBTOTAL	211	77	44	101	30	64	113	145	94	63	33	40	31	37	1,083	48	43	41	103
Unknown	5	1	3	2	0	3	2	3	8	1	0	0	3	2	33	0	0	1	1
TOTAL	216	78	47	103	30	67	115	148	102	64	33	40	34	39	1,116	48	43	42	104

(N = 1,353; Levels I, II, III, IV and diplomats)

The pattern of geographic distribution may be further analyzed by determining how many of the forty-six prefectures and how many of the eight regions are represented among higher civil servants. Table 7 summarizes Table 6 to obtain such a distribution in rank order. The number of prefectures represented varies substantially from one ministry to another, as if there had been some major differences in recruitment policy among the ministries. In

TABLE 7: BIRTHPLACE OF HIGHER CIVIL SERVANTS: PREFECTURAL AND REGIONAL DISTRIBUTION, BY MINISTRY (SUMMARY)

Core	Number of Prefectures	Number of Officials	Number of Regions	Periphery
Prime Minister's Office	41	211	7	
International Trade and Industry	36	145	7	
Transportation	36	94	7	
Agriculture and Forestry	34	113	7	
Finance	33	101	7	
	32	103	8	Ambassadors and Ministers
Justice	31	77	7	
Welfare	31	64	7	
Postal Services	29	63	7	
	23	48	8	National Personnel Authority
Foreign Affairs	22	44	7	
Economic Stabilization Board	22	37	7	
Labor	21	33	7	
Telecommunications	20	31	8	
Construction	19	40	8	
	19	43	7	Board of Audit
	18	41	8	Imperial Household Agency
Education	15	30	7	

(N = 1,318; Levels I, II, III, IV and diplomats)

reality, however, these variations are closely related to the number of higher civil servants in each ministry, and a careful analysis reveals a wide basis of origin for every ministry. Even in the Education Ministry, where recruitment appears narrowest, a proportion of thirty higher administrators from fifteen prefectures constitutes remarkable dispersal.

The number of regions represented in each ministry is more appropriate for this type of measurement, since it largely controls the varying sizes of the ministries. Also, for our purposes, regions are more meaningful than prefectures. While regions in Japan do not seem as politically important as those in some other nations, regions are more significantly related to Japan's social and economic development than prefectures. Yet the analysis on the basis of region shows equally remarkable dispersal. As presented in the fourth column of Table 7, the number of regions for each ministry is almost constant and shows an equally diversified pattern of geographic origin. Of the eight traditional regions, the one least often represented is Hokkaidō (not found in nine out of the eighteen basic units or "ministries"), where Japanese did not settle in any number until the late nineteenth century. Two other regions, Tōhoku and Shikoku, are missing from two ministries each, but otherwise all seven regions of old Japan supplied higher administrators to all the ministries.

It should be noted, however, that the number of higher civil servants varies considerably from one prefecture to another. As Table 6 shows, nearly 20 percent (197) are from Tokyo Metropolitan Prefecture alone, and no other single prefecture accounts for more than 6 percent. The highest among the remainder are Fukuoka (59), Hyōgo (53), Hiroshima (48), and Ōsaka (46). Extremely small figures, less than half of one percent, are found for Aomori (2), Tochigi (5), and Miyazaki (5). But it is also true that such wide variation is related to the differences in the prefectural population. The problem should be analyzed on the basis of the distribution of the Japanese population.

Most of the higher civil servants in this study were born in the decade following 1910, and entered the civil service in the 1930's. The first modern census in Japan was taken in 1920, midway between these two time points. The following analysis is therefore based on the 1920 census, emphasizing both the date of birth and the time of recruitment. Table 8 lists recruitment ratios for the prefectures, computed by dividing the prefectural proportions of higher civil servants by the prefectural proportions of the national population in 1920. For the purpose of comparison, parallel computations not shown here were made on the basis of different censuses. Each calculation, however, produced largely the same rank order of recruitment ratios, although there were considerable differences in the absolute ratios for rapidly growing prefectures.

The national average of recruitment ratios is, by definition, 1.00. The figure of 3.09 for Tokyo Metropolitan Prefecture thus indicates that higher administrators from this prefecture were about three times as numerous as the average for all the prefectures. At the other extreme, Aomori Prefecture, showing 0.04 for its recruitment ratio, provided only one twenty-fifth of the national average. The ratio for Tokyo is high since it supplied 20.6 percent of higher civil servants but had only 6.68 percent of the national population in 1920. Yet the small and sparsely populated prefecture of Tottori, with only 1.47 percent of the officials, ranks second in proportionate recruitment, since it had only 0.82 percent of the 1920 national population. By and large, these ratios fluctuate moderately except for a few at both ends of the list.

The degree of dispersion of these ratios can be systematically analyzed by examining its variance.[3] However, there is a simpler

[3] The pattern of a spread or dispersion can be expressed by simple numerical values. One of these is called "variance," while "standard deviation" is the square root of variance. Although they are not used here, use of these methods is explained in most textbooks of statistics, e.g., Blalock, *op.cit.*, pp. 67-75.

TABLE 8: Birthplace of Higher Civil Servants: Recruitment Ratios, by Prefecture*

Rank	Prefecture	Ratio	Rank	Prefecture	Ratio
1	Tōkyō	3.09	26	Nara	0.77
2	Tottori	1.79	27	Saitama	0.77
3	Yamanashi	1.71	28	Yamagata	0.75
4	Wakayama	1.70	29	Niigata	0.71
5	Hiroshima	1.49	30	Kōchi	0.68
6	Yamaguchi	1.35	31	Nagano	0.67
7	Okayama	1.35	32	Chiba	0.65
8	Ehime	1.31	33	Kanagawa	0.62
9	Kagawa	1.23	34	Gumma	0.61
10	Kyōto	1.20	35	Shiga	0.57
11	Toyama	1.19	36	Iwate	0.56
12	Mie	1.19	37	Fukui	0.56
13	Fukuoka	1.14	38	Aichi	0.55
14	Saga	1.13	39	Kumamoto	0.35
15	Ibaragi	1.11	40	Miyazaki	0.34
16	Ōsaka	1.03	41	Ishikawa	0.32
17	Kagoshima	1.02	42	Nagasaki	0.25
18	Shizuoka	1.01	43	Hokkaidō	0.23
19	Fukushima	0.99	44	Tochigi	0.21
20	Hyōgo	0.98	45	Akita	0.15
21	Tokushima	0.98	46	Aomori	0.04
22	Miyagi	0.95			
23	Shimane	0.95			
24	Ōita	0.90			
25	Gifu	0.81			

(N = 1,083; Core only; Levels I, II, III and IV)

* Recruitment Ratio =

$$\frac{\text{Proportion of higher civil servants originating from a given prefecture}}{\text{Proportion of the population of that prefecture in the total national population in 1920}}$$

method which illustrates the pattern more vividly for those not familiar with statistical analysis. Table 9 presents a distribution of the number of prefectures by recruitment ratio. More than half the prefectures have ratios between 0.60 and 1.39 and almost three-fourths fall between 0.50 and 1.49. In other words, recruitment from nearly three-fourths of the prefectures in Japan remained within the limits of 50 percent and 149 percent of the national average.

TABLE 9: BIRTHPLACE OF HIGHER CIVIL SERVANTS:
DISTRIBUTION OF THE NUMBER OF PREFECTURES, BY
RECRUITMENT RATIO

Range of Recruitment Ratios	Number of Prefectures	Proportion of Prefectures
0.90–1.09	9	19.6%
0.80–1.19	15	32.6%
0.70–1.29	21	45.7%
0.60–1.39	29	63.0%
0.50–1.49	34	73.9%
0.40–1.59	34	73.9%
0.30–1.69	37	80.4%
0.20–1.79	43	93.5%
0.10–1.89	44	95.7%
0.00–1.99 and over	46	100.0%

(N = 1,083; Core only; Levels I, II, III and IV)

Tables 6 through 9 indicate that postwar higher civil servants were recruited with reasonable uniformity from all parts of the country. This is somewhat remarkable, considering the lack of a formal or conscious policy of geographic dispersal in recruitment. Even in nations which have such a policy, geographic dispersal in recruitment is often difficult to achieve. According to Bendix's study, the Eastern and mid-Western states were substantially over-represented among higher civil servants of the United States federal government in 1940.[4] Warner and his associates also show a nearly identical form of overrepresentation in 1959, although their study is based upon a larger sample than Bendix's.[5]

Major reasons for such dispersal in Japan are not difficult to identify. One was the establishment of a system of higher civil service examinations (*kōtō bunkan shiken*) in the middle of the Meiji period. The other was the simultaneous creation of a uniform system of education throughout Japan, which provided young men with greater opportunity to obtain the higher education needed for competing in the civil service examinations.

URBAN-RURAL DISTRIBUTION

A factor which is closely related to region or prefecture is urbanization, and this is often regarded as one of the major variables in sociological and behavioral studies. In this study, some gross patterns of urban-rural distribution have already been indicated. The rank-order listing of the prefectural recruitment ratios (Table 8) suggests that recruitment from rural areas may be proportionately high. Except for Tokyo, the prefectures containing Japan's six largest cities appear unexpectedly low on the list, while three are below the national average: Tokyo, 3.09; Kyōto, 1.20; Ōsaka, 1.03; Hyōgo, 0.98; Kanagawa, 0.62; and Aichi, 0.55. On the other hand, Tottori, Yamanashi, Wakayama, and other predominantly rural prefectures appear high on the list.

A bureaucratic elite of rural origin would not be unusual in the Orient. Imperial China had a long tradition of gentry-scholar-bureaucrats who were mostly land-based and therefore rural.[6] Even

[4] Bendix, *op.cit.*, p. 24 (N = 234).

[5] W. Lloyd Warner, Paul P. Van Riper, Norman H. Martin, and Orvis F. Collins, *The American Federal Executive* (New Haven: Yale University Press, 1963), pp. 43, 327-29 (N = 10,851).

[6] P'an Kuang-tan and Fei Hsiao-t'ung, "City and Village: The Inequality of Opportunity," in Johanna M. Menzel, ed., *The Chinese Civil Service* (Boston: D. C. Heath, 1963), pp. 9-21.

in the United States, Bendix found that the single largest group (41.4 percent) among federal higher civil servants in 1940 were recruited primarily from rural areas with populations of less than 2,500.[7] A later U.S. study, however, shows more complex results. Although the single largest group (34 percent) in 1959 were from areas with populations of less than 2,500, recruitment ratios were highest in metropolitan areas.[8] In Japan, however, a different tradition would lead us to expect a predominantly urban elite in the bureaucracy. Removal of the samurai-warrior-bureaucrats from the countryside to castle towns in the sixteenth century made them urban by definition, and for the most part they remained in the towns and cities throughout the Tokugawa period.

It is difficult to make an urban-rural distinction in modern Japan. The steady trend toward urbanization within the confines of a small country, and the peculiarities of administrative districting, make it exceedingly hard to draw a clear line between urban and rural areas. Bendix used a population of 2,500 as the line of demarcation for the smallest (i.e., most rural) unit in his classification. This line approximated the division between Japanese villages and towns in the 1920's. In the present study, cities (*shi*) and towns (*machi*) are rather arbitrarily classified as urban and villages (*mura*) as rural.

Table 10 presents an urban-rural distribution by ministry of the origins of the 1949-1959 higher civil servants. A few major features may be immediately recognized. Nearly three-fourths of the core officials came from urban areas. Thus, predominantly urban origin is a major characteristic of postwar higher civil servants. The difference from one ministry to another tends to be small, and relatively little deviation is found within the core. On the other hand, a greater spread is found in the periphery, the National Personnel Authority having the highest proportion (90.3

[7] Bendix, *op.cit.*, p. 23.
[8] Warner et al., *op.cit.*, pp. 57-58, 333.

percent) and the Board of Audit the lowest (44.0 percent). As will be seen later, this is one of the many features which illustrate the heterogeneous nature of the periphery of the Japanese bureaucracy.

TABLE 10: PROPORTION OF URBAN-BORN HIGHER CIVIL SERVANTS, BY MINISTRY

Core	Proportion Urban-Born	Proportion Urban-Born	Periphery
		90.3%	National Personnel Authority
		88.4%	Imperial Household Agency
Education	85.7%		
Construction	82.6%		
Postal Services	80.0%		
		79.8%	Ambassadors and Ministers
Prime Minister's Office	76.3%		
Telecommunications	76.2%		
Finance	75.3%		
Economic Stabilization Board	75.0%		
Welfare	71.1%		
Agriculture and Forestry	70.4%		
Transportation	70.1%		
Foreign Affairs	69.2%		
International Trade and Industry	68.5%		
Labor	63.2%		
Justice	59.6%		
		44.0%	Board of Audit
Total (Core only)	72.6%		

(N = 938; Levels I, II, III, and diplomats)

When the same data are tabulated by survey year and position level, as set forth in Table 11, it is again evident that the general pattern of three-fourths urban and one-fourth rural largely persists regardless of year or level. A minor but consistent trend is a slight increase in the urban proportion from 1949 to 1959 (see the total column). Also, the proportions are inversely, though very weakly, related to position level. However, these trends are too minor to suggest a shift in recruitment or promotion policies, and appear to be natural results of the continuing urbanization of the nation as a whole.

TABLE 11: Proportion of Urban-Born Higher Civil Servants, by Year and Level

Year	Level				Total
	I	II	III	IV	
1949	75.6%	65.4%	69.4%	79.3%	76.7%
1954	73.0%	72.2%	77.4%	79.2%	78.0%
1959	68.4%	77.8%	73.1%	81.3%	78.9%
Total	72.4%	72.5%	73.0%	79.7%	77.7%

(N = 954; Core only)

There is an apparent contradiction between the data showing predominantly urban origin (Tables 10 and 11) and the data showing relatively low recruitment ratios for many prefectures with very large cities (Table 8). An explanation for this phenomenon is that the largest cities, except Tokyo, are often less important sources of recruitment than towns and medium-sized cities, which are scattered throughout the country. In fact, this is further evidence that the 1949-1959 higher administrators were widely recruited.

It should be stressed that the influence of geographic origin on values and attitudes seems much less significant than it is often thought to be. In twentieth century Japan, many individuals are physically as well as psychologically separated from their birthplaces for most of their lives so that the issue of prefectural origin or that of urban-rural difference has become less and less important for the development of their values and attitudes. This is especially true with respect to the impact of urban-rural difference upon the socialization of the bureaucratic elite. After the perfection of the higher civil service examinations system in the last decade of the nineteenth century, very few could become higher civil servants without a university education. Nearly all middle schools, higher schools, and universities were located in cities of considerable size, where most postwar higher civil servants spent a decade or more during their formative years.

Similarly attachment to the prefecture of origin appears to be sentimental rather than political. The regional allegiances of the past—notably in the early Meiji period—have largely disappeared, and it is unlikely that they will reemerge or will play some recognizable role. Uniform education, urbanization, and geographical mobility have mitigated the impact of regional ties on the values and attitudes of the Japanese people. Also the Japanese are highly homogeneous in ethnic origin, religion, and language, which in some countries tend to accentuate regional differences. Thus it is important not to overemphasize the implications of the preceding tables on the regional, prefectural, and urban-rural characteristics of the postwar Japanese higher civil servants.

AGE DISTRIBUTION

Although dispersed as to their birthplaces, the postwar higher civil servants tended to be about the same age and somewhat younger than might be expected in a society so sensitive to seniority. These features are particularly clear in comparison with civil servants in the United States. Figure 4 presents a comparative age distribution of Japanese and American administrators. Both U.S. distributions shown in the figure consist of groups about the same in size and rank as the Japanese group.[9] In Figure 4 the Jap-

[9] It should be noted, however, that the present study and both Bendix's and Kilpatrick's studies differ in selection criteria, sampling, and coverage (or response rate).

41

FIGURE 4: AGE DISTRIBUTIONS OF HIGHER CIVIL SERVANTS, JAPAN
AND THE UNITED STATES

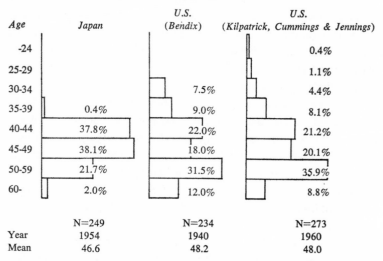

		U.S.	U.S.
Age	Japan	(Bendix)	(Kilpatrick, Cummings & Jennings)
-24			0.4%
25-29			1.1%
30-34		7.5%	4.4%
35-39	0.4%	9.0%	8.1%
40-44	37.8%	22.0%	21.2%
45-49	38.1%	18.0%	20.1%
50-59	21.7%	31.5%	35.9%
60-	2.0%	12.0%	8.8%
	N=249	N=234	N=273
Year	1954	1940	1960
Mean	46.6	48.2	48.0

SOURCES: Data on U.S. officials are from Bendix, *op.cit.*, p. 23, and Franklin P. Kilpatrick, Milton C. Cummings, Jr., and M. Kent Jennings, *The Image of the Federal Service*, ICPR, Survey Research Center, University of Michigan. The mean age of those reported by Bendix has been estimated from the data presented in his study. Figures for Japan include those in Levels I, II, and III in the core.

anese distribution is much more concentrated than either of the U.S. distributions. Important differences are seen in both the lower and the higher age groups (39 and below, 60 and over), where the Japanese distribution shows very small proportions. Also, the average age of the Japanese group is appreciably lower than the comparable groups in the United States. Although there is a question of comparability which cannot be readily solved in a case of this sort, these data clarify some of the gross differences between Japanese and American higher civil servants.

A distribution of ages by survey years and position levels, however, shows that the average age of the Japanese administrators was steadily increasing during the survey period (1949-1959). As shown in Table 12, the average age for those in Level IV and above increased 2.6 years between 1949 and 1954, and 1.3 years between 1954 and 1959 (see the total column). The increase is seen at every level in every interval, ranging from 0.7 to 2.9 years. This is one of the most conspicuous chronological changes found in the data on postwar higher civil servants, and the reasons for it are not apparent. One hypothesis is that the Occupation purge removed a sizable group of higher civil servants so that the average age was reduced in earlier survey years but was returning to a "normal" level in later years. Another hypothesis is that the postwar decline in the social and political prestige of higher civil service positions has made it less easy to secure attractive positions upon leaving the civil service, so that senior administrators tend to postpone retirement somewhat longer than in the past. While the present tabulation is inadequate to prove or disprove these hypotheses, an analysis in the latter part of this study lends some support for both of them.

TABLE 12: AVERAGE AGE OF HIGHER CIVIL SERVANTS, BY YEAR AND LEVEL

	Level				
Year	*I*	*II*	*III*	*IV*	*Total*
1949	49.2	44.2	43.9	39.8	41.0
1954	49.9	46.2	45.8	42.1	43.6
1959	51.8	48.2	48.2	43.4	44.9
Total	50.3	46.4	45.8	41.9	43.1

(N = 1,089; Core only)

Table 12 also indicates that age is closely correlated with position level, and that there exists an age difference of three or five years from one level to the next, except between Levels II and III. The absence of such a difference between these two levels is primarily due to the special character of Level III. Whenever the two organizational units co-exist in a ministry or agency, divisions are always placed under bureaus. In practice, however, divisions and bureaus are frequently mutually exclusive units of organization. In such cases chiefs of division (Level III) tend to be directly responsible to vice-ministers and directors (Level I). Thus men in Level III are often likely to be about as old as those in Level II (chiefs of bureau). It is a reflection of this circumstance that Level II and Level III positions are assigned to the same pay group, while other levels constitute separate pay groups.[10] It is also the case that some of those in Level III positions are engaged in rather specialized tasks, and tend to remain in such posts for longer periods. This topic of age and position level is important in a bureaucracy where seniority rules are said to be rigidly observed, and it will be further discussed in Chapter 5.

Greater irregularities in age are found when the same data are tabulated by ministry. As shown in Table 13 the average ages in the periphery cluster at the upper end, and those in the core at the lower end. Within each category there is considerable spread in age. The range between maximum and minimum average ages is seven years, in both the core and the periphery. However, the difference from one unit to another in the periphery is larger than in the core, resulting in greater heterogeneity in the periphery as a whole than in the core as a whole. The very high average ages for officials in the Imperial Household Agency, the Board of Audit, and diplomats are related to special features of their careers, which will also be discussed in Chapter 5.

The age variation in the core is apparently affected by at least two major factors, which are sometimes supplementary and sometimes contradictory. These are the history of a ministry and the relationship between the function of a ministry and post-retirement job opportunities. New ministries in Japan are usually created either by dividing an existing ministry or by expanding sub-minis-

[10] The National Personnel Authority Rule, Article 9-8, Attached Table No. 1.

TABLE 13: AVERAGE AGE OF HIGHER CIVIL SERVANTS, BY MINISTRY

Core	Average Age	Average Age	Periphery
		55.8	Ambassadors and Ministers
		54.7	Imperial Household Agency
		51.5	Board of Audit
Justice	50.5		
Construction	49.0		
Education	48.5		
		48.2	National Personnel Authority
Foreign Affairs	48.2		
Welfare	47.6		
Prime Minister's Office	47.0		
Agriculture and Forestry	47.0		
Postal Services	47.0		
Transportation	46.7		
Labor	45.6		
International Trade and Industry	45.2		
Telecommunications	44.8		
Finance	43.6		
Economic Stabilization Board	43.2		
Total (Core only)	46.8		

(N = 1,001; Levels I, II, III and diplomats)

terial units of different ministries and combining them into a new ministry. In either case, the change tends to upgrade the position levels of administrators already in charge of the particular functions involved in a reorganization, and to cause the promotion of men in the older units to higher ranks in the new supervisory positions. These new positions are likely to be held by slightly younger persons, because a new ministry tends to be less prestigious and less powerful at least in its early years. It is noteworthy that all

45

ministries created since 1945, except Construction, have average ages below the core average.

The second factor is probably the more significant. Low average ages are found in both the Finance Ministry, created in 1869, and the International Trade and Industry Ministry, created in 1925. In these instances, the low average ages reflect early retirement opportunities due to attractive offers primarily from private business.[11] Senior administrators in these ministries acquire both specialized knowledge and personal influence which are useful in business and elsewhere, and they tend to leave the government at an early age. Conversely, other ministries such as Welfare and Education have high average ages because of less attractive post-retirement prospects. In spite of the remarkable scale of construction and building in the postwar Japanese economy, those in the Construction Ministry did not fare any better. Traditionally, Construction has hardly been regarded as a promising career field by university graduates. Also the industry itself has seldom recruited retiring civil servants. Despite economic changes, these conditions apparently still prevail.

The Justice Ministry has the highest average age in the core. One reason is that private practice of law in Japan, the outside career which Justice officials would most naturally seek, has not offered, at least until recent years, the kind of prestige and financial rewards long enjoyed by American or British attorneys. Another reason is that for policy reasons and by custom most higher administrative posts in the Justice Ministry are filled by men with long experience as public procurators, who normally follow career patterns quite different from administrators in other ministries. Their pay scale is separate from those in other ministries, and

[11] There are some laws and ordinances in Japan which control conflicts of interests (e.g., The National Public Service Law, Article 103, par. 2). In practice, however, restrictions upon post-retirement employment appear to have been leniently applied.

their careers tend to resemble those of judges.[12] By the time they reach high positions in the ministry, they are thus substantially older than administrators in other ministries.

FATHERS AND FATHERS-IN-LAW

The parental backgrounds of the 1949-1959 higher civil servants are recorded only to a limited extent in published biographical sources. The following analysis, therefore, is limited to those who were related by birth or marriage to the highest strata in Japanese society. These sources always provide the name of the father and that of the father-in-law in the column for each individual higher civil servant listed, but they do not indicate the occupations or positions of the parents unless they achieved considerable prominence. Conversely, those parents who attained national eminence are always identified in their own columns as well as in those of their sons or their sons-in-law. The following tables show the proportion of the 1949-1959 higher civil servants whose fathers or fathers-in-law were found eminent in either one of these two types of columns.

Two broad categories of classification are used. Those who are "politically prominent" include cabinet ministers, Diet members, prefectural or colonial governors, Justices of the Supreme Court or the colonial high courts, officers of major political parties and higher civil servants with the rank of bureau chief or above. The second category is broader than the first; those who are "prominent" include generals, admirals, officers of major corporations, members of the former peerage, distinguished writers and scholars, and merchants with high incomes as well as the "politically prominent." On the other hand, prefectural or municipal assemblymen, middle-school principals, medical doctors, and lawyers (unless nationally known) are excluded from both categories.

[12] The Salaries of Public Procurators Law, Article 2 and Attached Table.

Table 14 shows a distribution by ministry of higher civil servants with "prominent" fathers or fathers-in-law. The ministries are ranked according to the sums of the two types of proportions. Although these sums include some duplications (officials with both prominent fathers and prominent fathers-in-law are counted twice), they serve as general indicators of eminent parental backgrounds. A notable feature of Table 14 is a relatively extensive variation

TABLE 14: PROPORTION OF HIGHER CIVIL SERVANTS WITH PROMINENT FATHERS AND FATHERS-IN-LAW, BY MINISTRY

Core	"Prominent" Fathers	"Prominent" Fathers-in-Law	Periphery
	33.3%	18.5%	Imperial Household Agency
Education	17.4%	26.1%	
	11.5%	20.2%	Ambassadors and Ministers
Foreign Affairs	13.8%	17.2%	
Prime Minister's Office	15.3%	15.3%	
Finance	11.0%	19.5%	
Economic Stabilization Board	3.4%	24.1%	
International Trade and Industry	11.3%	11.3%	
Postal Services	13.3%	8.9%	
Justice	9.5%	6.3%	
	9.1%	6.1%	National Personnel Authority
Transportation	2.9%	11.4%	
Telecommunications	4.8%	9.5%	
Labor	4.8%	9.5%	
Agriculture and Forestry	7.2%	6.0%	
Welfare	6.1%	4.1%	
	3.6%	3.6%	Board of Audit
Construction	3.6%	0.0%	
Total (Core only)	10.0%	12.1%	

(N = 1,002; Levels I, II, III, and diplomats)

among ministries. These differences in proportion of prominent fathers or fathers-in-law seem to be related to several factors.

One is the relative prestige of each ministry, a motivational element which memoirs and biographies show to have considerable influence upon career choices by candidates for the civil service. The diplomatic service (the Foreign Affairs Ministry and the diplomatic corps) appeared to be a highly preferred choice of candidates, although the Finance Ministry and the International Trade and Industry Ministry probably were equally attractive to candidates with somewhat different interests and aptitudes. The Economic Stabilization Board was a postwar offshoot of these two ministries, and its proportions are similarly high. At the other extreme are the Welfare Ministry and the Construction Ministry, whose low proportions of prominent parents coincide with their relatively low prestige.

A second factor is the variation in recruitment policy. The Imperial Household Agency, for example, has traditionally preferred to recruit sons of the peerage (now disestablished) or of distinguished families. The 1949-1959 officials of this agency included a son of a former prime minister and descendants of elite feudal families such as the Tokugawa and Matsudaira (all former peers).

A third factor is marriage. Nearly all the 1949-1959 higher civil servants apparently married through the traditional form of arrangement by their parents. In such circumstances, it was natural that those in the upper social strata tended to intermarry. Table 14 indicates some relationship between the figures for prominent fathers and those for prominent fathers-in-law. In addition, prospective higher civil servants tended to marry daughters of families which were of higher social status than their own, because of the popular belief that they were already virtually assured of rapid rise on the social ladder. "Marrying up" is perhaps most common in the diplomatic service and the Finance Ministry, and our data support such a supposition. The unusually high proportion of prominent fathers-in-law for the Economic Stabilization Board also falls into this pattern. It is significant to note that on the average the 1949-1959 higher civil servants more often had prominent fathers-in-law than prominent fathers.

The Education Ministry is an exception to the above analysis. This ministry has in general lacked prestige with the public and with applicants for the civil service. There seems to be little reason to believe that it has favored sons of distinguished families any more than other ministries. However, our data suggest strong ties, marital or nonmarital, with prominent families. The reasons for this characteristic are not clear.

Table 15 presents a distribution by ministry of higher civil servants with "politically prominent" fathers and fathers-in-law. By and large, the pattern is parallel to that in Table 14, suggesting similar reasons for the distribution of sons of politically prominent families among ministries. Also, they were on the average more frequently related to politically prominent families by marriage than by birth, again suggesting the general pattern of "marrying up" among higher administrators. Minor differences between these two tables are that the Education Ministry ranks highest of all in Table 15, while the Finance Ministry and the Economic Stabilization Board have dropped significantly.

Perhaps a more significant feature in Table 15 is the overall smallness of the proportions of those with politically prominent fathers and fathers-in-law (3.0 percent and 4.0 percent respectively) for all the ministries. It is difficult, therefore, to establish a strong linkage between higher civil servants and politically outstanding parents in Japan. Also, in Table 15 the variation among the ministries is almost negligible, especially in comparison with Table 14, owing to the general smallness of proportions. It is difficult to draw strong inferences from the ranking of ministries in Table 15. In other words, there is clearly a limitation in explaining these concentrations by the relative prestige or by the recruit-

TABLE 15: PROPORTION OF HIGHER CIVIL SERVANTS WITH POLITICALLY
PROMINENT FATHERS AND FATHERS-IN-LAW, BY MINISTRY

Core	Politically "Prominent" Fathers	Politically "Prominent" Fathers-in-Law	Periphery
Education	0.0%	17.4%	
Prime Minister's Office	5.3%	7.1%	
	7.4%	3.7%	Imperial Household Agency
	5.8%	4.8%	Ambassadors and Ministers
Foreign Affairs	3.4%	6.9%	
Justice	6.3%	3.2%	
	6.1%	3.0%	National Personnel Authority
Postal Services	2.2%	4.4%	
International Trade and Industry	3.1%	3.1%	
Finance	3.7%	1.2%	
Labor	0.0%	4.8%	
Transportation	0.0%	4.3%	
Construction	3.6%	0.0%	
	3.6%	0.0%	Board of Audit
Economic Stabilization Board	0.0%	3.4%	
Agriculture and Forestry	1.2%	1.2%	
Welfare	2.0%	0.0%	
Telecommunications	0.0%	0.0%	
Total (Core only)	3.0%	4.0%	

(N = 1,002; Levels I, II, III, and diplomats)

ment policy of the various ministries. Such a limitation is to some extent found in the table on prominent parents, but it is most clearly seen in the table on politically prominent parents.

Similarly, the very high proportions of prominent, especially politically prominent, parents of higher civil servants in the Education Ministry cautions us against overemphasis upon a thesis of ministerial favoritism in recruitment, transfer, and promotion on the basis of family background. A certain degree of such favoritism may be unavoidable in any bureaucracy, and our data do suggest such a tendency in the Japanese case. Yet its extent appears limited, and it becomes necessary to turn to a different type of analysis of the parental backgrounds of the 1949-1959 higher administrators.

Table 16 sets forth a distribution by position level of higher civil servants with eminent fathers and fathers-in-law. A major implication of this table is that position level and parental status are almost unrelated (or independent in statistical terminology). The proportions with prominent fathers and fathers-in-law (the upper half of the table) are approximately 10.0 percent with slight deviation throughout the levels. The distribution for prominent fathers is only slightly correlated with position level, but the pattern clearly breaks down in the case of prominent fathers-in-law. The proportions for politically prominent parents (the lower half of the table) are appreciably less than the former. Although for fathers the distribution is positive (meaning the higher the level, the higher the proportion), its degree of correlation is very small. Similarly, the distribution of politically prominent fathers-in-law hardly supports the thesis of favoritism in promotion on the basis of family background.

TABLE 16: PROPORTION OF HIGHER CIVIL SERVANTS WITH EMINENT
FATHERS AND FATHERS-IN-LAW, BY POSITION LEVEL

	Level				
Parent	*I*	*II*	*III*	*IV*	*Total*
Prominent:					
Fathers	13.6%	9.8%	8.7%	9.3%	9.5%
Fathers-in-Law	9.6%	14.7%	9.7%	8.9%	9.7%
Politically Prominent:					
Fathers	5.6%	2.8%	2.0%	1.1%	1.5%
Fathers-in-Law	1.6%	5.2%	5.1%	1.8%	2.3%

(N = 1,090; Core only)

In short, it is difficult to detect a strong influence of parental background upon the pattern of promotion of postwar higher administrators. Conversely, our data suggest that something other than social standing by birth or marriage is more meaningfully related to the advancement of these officials. This is perhaps what one would expect in a nation where all candidates for the executive branch of higher civil service have been required to take stiff competitive examinations. The qualifications for such examinations were determined by education. Family status, no matter how high or low, neither guaranteed nor prevented entrance into the civil service.

Yet it would be unrealistic to deny the influence of family status entirely. Assignments to particular ministries, if not promotions, appear substantially related to parental background as shown in Tables 14 and 15. Such a feature is understandable in view of the importance traditionally attributed to family status in Japan. Furthermore, family prominence might have given more substantive advantages to prospective candidates by providing them with stronger motivation and superior financial resources for obtaining the kind of education needed for the civil service examinations. It is, for instance, clear that among postwar higher civil servants the proportion originating from the highest strata of Japanese society is unquestionably greater than the proportion of such families in the national population as a whole. While approximately 10 percent of the 1949-1959 higher administrators had "prominent" parents, less than half of one percent, if liberally estimated, of the national population belonged to this category. Although data such as those presented here leave ample room for doubt in determining the overall social mobility of high civil servants (it may be very high or very low), there is little question that these highest strata have supplied a disproportionately large number of higher civil servants.

CLASS STATUS

In traditional Japan, class was more important than family in recruitment of officials. Until the Meiji Restoration of 1868, the Japanese people were divided into four classes, i.e., warriors (*bushi*), farmers (*nōmin*), artisans (*kōnin*), and merchants (*shōnin*), ranking legally and socially in that order. The three lower classes were ineligible for government office. The warriors were concurrently bureaucrats, and they monopolized public office under successive shogunates. Paralleling the warriors were court nobles (*kuge*), an extra-feudal class that held all positions in the then impotent imperial bureaucracy.

The Restoration began by ignoring the traditional demarcation between noble and warrior, and by relaxing the link between class status and occupation. The initial post-Restoration system included four classes: *kōzoku* (the imperial family and its relatives); *kazoku* (or peerage, including former feudal lords, court nobles, and other distinguished individuals); *shizoku* (most of the former *bushi* or warriors); and *heimin* (or commoners, including all the others). At the same time, the Meiji government rapidly eliminated legal distinctions among the classes, especially between *shizoku* and *heimin*. Thus during the first decade of the Meiji period (1868-1877), most legal distinctions were abolished, although these terms themselves officially remained until the end of World War II.

Social changes were more gradual, however, and *shizoku* (samurai) continued to dominate the civil service for many years after the Restoration. Yet the proportion of *shizoku* among public servants declined quite rapidly, thus reflecting institutional changes. One investigator found that the percentage of *shizoku* among "civil servants" dropped by 16 percent in six years (1876-1882).[13] Another concluded that even before the end of

---

[13] Fukuchi Shigetaka, *Shizoku to samurai ishiki* (Tokyo: Shunjūsha, 1946), p. 333.

the Meiji period (1912), a majority of "higher officials" were *heimin* (commoners).[14] Although the terms "civil servants" and "higher officials" in these studies do not precisely correspond to our term "higher civil servant" as defined in Chapter 2, the general rise of *heimin* is undeniable.

The class distribution of the 1949-1959 higher civil servants is unknown, since postwar biographical sources no longer record class status. The same information disappeared from the *Official Gazette* (*Kampō*) lists of national university graduates and civil service candidates as far back as 1918. However, it seems safe to conclude that the earlier trend of the rise of *heimin* continued. As late as 1937, 72.4 percent of "higher civil servants" (a group roughly equivalent to the group of higher civil servants defined in this study) were *heimin*,[15] and it appears that a majority of postwar higher civil servants were not from the former samurai (*shizoku*) or any higher classes.

There are several other noteworthy social characteristics of the postwar higher civil servants. To begin with, it is clear that very few of the 1949-1959 higher civil servants were following hereditary occupations. Less than 3 percent (see Table 16) were sons or sons-in-law of influential government officials (bureau chiefs or above, justices of high courts, diplomats, etc.). Conceivably, many of them might have been related to minor officials or public employees (clerks, policemen, teachers, etc.), but there is no evidence during this period that high civil service posts were held by successive generations to any significant degree.[16]

14 Asō Makoto, "Meijiki ni okeru kōtō kyōiku shokikan no erīto keisei kinō ni kansuru kenkyū," *Kyōikugaku kenkyū*, Vol. 30, No. 2 (May 1963), pp. 114, 118, 121.

15 Inoki Masamichi, "The Civil Bureaucracy: Japan," in Robert E. Ward and Dankwart A. Rustow, eds., *Political Modernization in Japan and Turkey* (Princeton: Princeton University Press, 1964), p. 296.

16 On the basis of his and Mannari's data (Inoki, *op.cit.*, p. 298), Inoki concludes that "[the] civil service in Japan is in a manner hereditary."

On the contrary, our data indicate a substantial degree of upward social mobility. The higher civil service has possessed great prestige in Japan. Biographical sources themselves provide some evidence. While virtually all of those in Level III or above are recorded in standard biographical sources, only a few of their parents are included in their own right in contemporary or earlier editions. Another indication of rising social status is seen in marriage. Entry into the higher civil service automatically raised an official's prospective social standing, and consequently improved his chance of marrying the daughter of a prominent family. "Marrying up" is most evident among those who became ambassadors, ministers, and higher officials in the Finance Ministry and the Economic Stabilization Board.

According to our data, one higher civil servant out of every ten was related to a "prominent" family either by birth or marriage, and less than one in twenty was related to a "politically prominent" family. In view of such proportions and the wide variety of occupations included in both categories, it is obvious that the upper bureaucracy was not dominated by any identifiable "higher" class or single influential group. Similarly, the broad geographic basis shown earlier suggests that the social basis of recruitment was reasonably widespread. On the other hand, it is difficult to believe that the bulk of these higher administrators originated in the "lower" class. As mentioned already, the highest strata supplied a disproportionately large, though not dominating, number of higher civil servants. Moreover, economic factors discourage such a supposition. As we shall see in Chapter 4, practically all the 1949-1959 civil servants were college graduates; the cost of col-

---

Depending upon the time and the coverage of a survey, it should be expected that data may support the hereditary thesis. It should be noted, however, that the same article stresses class mobility (rise of *heimin*), and that his definition of "public officials" is different from our definition of "politically prominent" persons.

lege education was such, however, that sons of poor families were largely excluded.[17] Scholarships and part-time job opportunities were not sufficient to alter this situation materially. On balance, it seems that a majority of higher civil servants probably came from what may be broadly called the middle class.

[17] See, for instance, Asō Makoto, "Meiji zenki (yōranki) kōtō kyōiku no shokeitai to sono erīto keisei kōka ni kansuru kenkyū," *Nihon Ikueikai kenkyū kiyō*, Vol. 1 (May 1963), Appendix 1, p. 71; Inoki, *op.cit.*, pp. 295-296.

CHAPTER 4

Educational Backgrounds

EDUCATION is a critical issue in any description or discussion of Japanese higher civil servants. The proportion of higher administrators with a university education is remarkably high, even in comparison with major Western bureaucracies, although the modern Japanese university system dates only from the last quarter of the nineteenth century.[1] In addition, the university training of Japanese higher civil servants is remarkably homogeneous and exhibits unusual concentration in terms of subjects studied and schools attended. Such features and the inferences drawn from them have been subjects of endless controversy among critics of the Japanese system.

The 1949-1959 higher civil servants had completed their formal education before the Occupation reorganization of the Japanese educational system at the end of World War II. Hence their

[1] Although an exact comparison is difficult owing to institutional differences, the following data are available:

Nation	Proportion Attending College	N	Year
United States*	87.7%	243	1940
United Kingdom	86.2%	332	1950
Japan	99.2%	249	1954

* Franklin P. Kilpatrick, Milton C. Cummings, Jr., and M. Kent Jennings, *The Image of the Federal Service*, ICPR, Survey Research Center, University of Michigan, shows that 84.2% of the 1960 federal executives attended college. It should be noted, however, that this study was based upon a sample of its own design, and that 37.7% went to the post-graduate levels.

From Bendix, *op.cit.*, p. 39; and R. K. Kelsall, *Higher Civil Servants in Britain from 1870 to the Present Day* (London: Routledge and Kegan Paul, 1955), p. 136.

educational backgrounds must be understood in terms of prewar conditions. The school system these administrators attended was pieced together between 1868 and 1889 and steadily expanded thereafter. In the first years of the Meiji period, American influence in education was dominant, but by the late 1880's, European influence—primarily German, secondarily French—had become paramount, especially above the elementary level.

Most of the administrators in this study were born in the first quarter of the twentieth century, and by that time the basic pattern of the school system was clearly laid out. After 1908, six years of elementary school (*shō gakkō*) was compulsory for all Japanese children. Above this level, students were divided among several educational "ladders" leading to quite different careers. The most difficult and by far the most promising one, which may be called the "academic" ladder, led through five years of middle school (*chū gakkō*), three years of higher school (*kōtō gakkō*), and three years of university (*daigaku*), followed, if desired, by postgraduate study. This path or a close variant of it had to be followed if a student was to have much hope of entering higher administrative positions in the government, in large corporations, or in the academic world. Other ladders, demanding less rigorous competition and less intensive training, generally led to inferior positions in society, and it was very difficult to switch from one of these to the academic ladder.

In effect, the range of careers open to a student depended largely upon his academic achievements and upon personal or parental decisions made no later than at the age of seventeen or eighteen. This was especially true of those who subsequently became higher civil servants. Applicants without at least two years of university education were rarely able to pass the prewar higher civil service examinations (*kōtō bunkan shiken*), which were required for all except technicians, teachers, and certain other exempt categories. As will be shown presently, the overwhelming majority of postwar higher administrators came from the imperial universities, which admitted few students who were not graduates of higher schools. Higher schools, in turn, admitted few who were not graduates of middle schools. In fact only a very small proportion of the total number of middle school graduates in any given prewar year—usually about 5 percent—were able to gain admission to higher schools.[2]

Since the total enrollment in higher schools (even after the expansion following World War I) was not much larger than that of the imperial universities, it was clearly easier for a higher school graduate to enter a university than for a middle school graduate to enter a higher school. In other words, the higher school entrance examination was usually the most difficult hurdle for a prospective higher civil servant, short of the higher civil service examinations themselves. It is, therefore, appropriate to start with higher schools in tracing the educational backgrounds of the 1949-1959 higher civil servants.

HIGHER SCHOOL

The prewar Japanese higher schools (*kōtō gakkō*) were patterned after the upper level of the German *Gymnasium* and the French *lycée*. They corresponded very roughly to an American liberal arts

[2] The following were the numbers of students enrolled at these levels in two sample years:

Year	Middle Schools	Higher Schools	Universities
1919	166,616 (100%)	7,558 (4%)	7,337 (4%)
1929	348,584 (100%)	20,256 (6%)	38,457 (11%)*

* The figure for university students is larger than that for higher-school students because after 1919 it included newly recognized private universities, whose students generally attended preparatory schools other than higher schools.

From Kindai Nihon Kyōiku Seido Shiryō Hensankai, comp., *Kindai Nihon kyōiku seido shiryō*, Vol. 35 (Tokyo: Kōdansha, 1959), pp. 254-255, 316-317.

college, not to an American high school. Higher schools usually had two sections (*ka*), dividing students into two main groups: those planning to specialize at a university in law, the humanities, or the social sciences, and those planning to study medicine, engineering, or the natural sciences. Within each section, students were further divided according to the foreign languages in which they majored. However, students in both sections were required to take certain courses in the social sciences, the natural sciences, foreign languages, and the humanities, although the allocation of hours for each of these fields varied considerably depending upon the sections and language groups to which they belonged.

Prior to 1919, there were only eight higher schools in the whole nation, which were designated by number in sequence of establishment. Between 1919 and 1923, seventeen more (designated not by number but by name of city or locality) were established, making a total of twenty-five operated by the national government (the Education Ministry). Also, three prefectural and three private higher schools were created in Japan proper in the 1920's, while two others were established in the colonies (at Taipei in 1921; and at Port Arthur in 1940), making a grand total of thirty-three. These higher schools were always small. Even the largest rarely graduated more than 400 students a year for all fields combined. But there was considerable variation in prestige. Most highly regarded were the eight "number" (*nambā*) schools established between 1877 and 1908, of which the First Higher School in Tokyo was generally considered the best of all.

Table 17 shows a distribution by higher school of the 1949-1959 higher civil servants who attended imperial universities (90.4 percent of all those in Level III and above in the core). More than a quarter graduated from the First Higher School, and the seven other numbered schools together accounted for another three-tenths. Thus the eight numbered schools produced more than half of those who attended imperial universities. All the unnumbered

61

schools together, public or private, accounting for one-fifth of the total, produced fewer than the First Higher School alone. However, higher school background is unknown for a quarter of the total group. Some of these presumably graduated from higher schools whose alumni directories are not available, or from other preparatory schools.[3] At any rate, it is significant to find such a skewed

TABLE 17: Higher School Background
of Higher Civil Servants Who Attended Imperial
Universities

Higher School	Proportion	Total
Numbered Higher Schools:		
No. 1 (Tokyo)	25.8%	
No. 5 (Kumamoto)	6.0%	
No. 8 (Nagoya)	6.0%	
No. 3 (Kyōto)	5.1%	
No. 4 (Kanazawa)	4.9%	
No. 6 (Okayama)	3.3%	
No. 2 (Sendai)	2.9%	
No. 7 (Kagoshima)	1.1%	
Subtotal for Numbered Schools		55.1%
Unnumbered Higher Schools:		
Fukuoka	1.9%	
Ōsaka	1.6%	
Mito	1.6%	
Tokyo	1.5%	
Urawa	1.4%	
Naniwa (Ōsaka Prefectural)	1.2%	
Matsue	1.0%	
Shizuoka	0.8%	
All Others	9.0%	
Subtotal for Unnumbered Schools		20.0%
Unknown		24.9%
Total		100.0%

(N = 732; Levels I, II, and III; Core only)

[3] Some of the 24.9 percent whose background is unknown in Table 17 seem to have attended higher schools for which only limited data are avail-

distribution, since all higher schools were ostensibly equal in academic standards and nearly equal in size.[4]

In view of the sizable number of First Higher School graduates, it is relevant to examine their distribution within the upper bureaucracy. Table 18 presents the proportion by ministry of First Higher School graduates among all the higher civil servants in Level III and above. The figure varies considerably, ranging from less than 10 percent to more than 50 percent. High proportions—approximately a third—are found in the two ministries which were generally preferred by civil service applicants: Foreign Affairs and Finance. The highest percentage is seen in the Economic Stabilization Board, a postwar organization staffed largely by persons formerly in Finance and in International Trade and Industry. On the other hand, very low proportions are found in the Postal Services and the Telecommunications Ministries, which had been combined as the Communications Ministry (*Teishin Shō*) before the war.

In the periphery, the proportions of First Higher School graduates tend to be higher than in the core. One reason for this is probably the general age difference between core and peripheral officials. As shown in Table 13, the latter tended to be older than the former in the 1949-1959 period. The earlier in time, the more im-

---

able. However, a recognizable minority appear to have graduated from schools other than higher schools, such as national and private technical and vocational higher schools (*senmon gakkō*), military academies and other universities. See, for instance, *Tōdai jinmei roku: Kanchō hen* (Tokyo: Tōdai Sotsugyōsei Meibo Hensan Iinkai, 1962).

[4] The enrollments of higher schools were not exactly equal. The following are the numbers of graduates of the "numbered" higher schools in 1935:

No. 1	No. 2	No. 3	No. 4	No. 5	No. 6	No. 7	No. 8
369	204	271	201	246	242	191	228

From the Ministry of Education, Secretariat, Secretary Section, comp., *Dai Nihon Teikoku Mombu Shō dai rokujū san nempō*, p. 155.

TABLE 18: PROPORTION OF FIRST HIGHER SCHOOL GRADUATES
AMONG HIGHER CIVIL SERVANTS, BY MINISTRY

Core	Proportion	Proportion	Periphery
		53.6%	Board of Audit
		40.2%	Ambassadors and Ministers
Economic Stabilization Board	37.9%		
		37.0%	Imperial Household Agency
Foreign Affairs	34.5%		
Finance	32.9%		
Justice	31.7%		
Education	30.4%		
International Trade and Industry	29.9%		
Prime Minister's Office	21.8%		
		21.2%	National Personnel Authority
Labor	19.0%		
Welfare	18.4%		
Transportation	18.1%		
Agriculture and Forestry	14.5%		
Construction	14.3%		
Postal Services	11.1%		
Telecommunications	9.5%		
Total (Core only)	23.3%		

(N = 1,002; Levels I, II, III and diplomats)

portant the relative position of the First Higher School, and being older, peripheral officials were more likely to be First graduates. Another noticeable feature is that the proportion tends to vary more in the periphery than in the core. The difference, for instance, between the Imperial Household Agency and the National Personnel Authority is scarcely comparable to any difference between two adjoining ministries in the core ordering. The greater variation in higher school background also illustrates the heterogeneous composition of those in the periphery.

It should be noted, however, that the sizable variation in Table 18 cannot be explained solely by age factors or the relative prestige of each ministry. In the core, the proportion for Education is unexpectedly high while in the periphery the highest proportion is found in the Board of Audit. The situation in Education is similar to the case of parental background and is difficult to explain. The high proportion in the Board of Audit is also perplexing since it exceeds that of the diplomats, for whom a First Higher School background was popularly thought to be essential. In order to explore these questions further, it is necessary to analyze the data in a different manner.

Table 19 presents a distribution by survey year and position level of First Higher School graduates among the postwar higher civil servants in this study. Before discussing the relationship between position level and higher school background it is necessary to examine certain deviating features in Table 19. First, the substantially lower proportion for Level I in 1949 reflects the impact of the Allied Occupation. This group included vice-ministers, directors of agencies, and other high-ranking officials many of whom were purged or resigned through fear of being purged. At the same time, virtually all First Higher School graduates in the bureaucracy were also Tokyo University graduates, and American efforts to encourage promotion of those from other universities resulted in a reduction of First Higher School graduates in Level I. Second, the lowest proportion of all is found for Level IV in 1959. This seems to be due to a different chronological factor. Nearly all of those in Level IV in 1959 graduated from higher schools after 1929, and by that time, there were thirty-two instead of eight higher schools. First Higher School graduates then faced about three times as many competitors both for admission to outstanding imperial universities and in the higher civil service examinations. The same factor is also responsible for a steady decline of the total proportion (see the total column) during the survey years.

So far as the relationship between position level and higher

TABLE 19: Proportion of First Higher School Graduates Among Higher Civil Servants, by Year and Level

Year	Level				Total
	I	*II*	*III*	*IV*	
1949	13.0%	26.3%	18.6%	19.0%	19.4%
1954	28.2%	28.0%	19.6%	16.7%	18.5%
1959	32.5%	21.9%	25.0%	7.1%	11.8%
Total	24.0%	25.1%	20.8%	14.6%	16.8%

(N = 1,090; Core only)

school background is concerned, Table 19 shows only a weak correlation. In the 1949 group the relation is highly disturbed, but in the 1954 group, a clear and positive though weak association emerges. For the 1959 group, again the overall relationship is positive, although it breaks down between Levels II and III. This pattern may be summarized by omitting the data for 1949, when the impact of an unusual political situation was still apparent, and by combining the data for 1954 and 1959. Then, the proportions for the four levels become 30.4 percent, 24.6 percent, 22.2 percent, and 13.9 percent respectively. This summary measure suggests a moderate overall relationship between higher school background and position level.

In discussing Table 18, we referred to the unusually high proportions of First Higher School graduates in the Education Ministry and the Board of Audit. A partial explanation lies in this modest association between position level and higher school background. Generally, this relationship varies considerably from ministry to ministry and creates a different degree of concentration of First graduates in the upper levels of each ministry. Though not presented here, the degrees of clustering at the upper levels in these two units are very high, thus resulting in the very high proportions of First graduates for the Education Ministry and the Board of Audit.

Such a relationship, however, does not substantiate the widespread belief in Japan that it was "necessary" to attend the First Higher School and then Tokyo Imperial University in order to reach a high position in the bureaucracy. Even in Level I, less than one-fourth of the 1949-1959 higher civil servants were graduates of the First Higher School. Among those holding the very highest civil service positions, administrative vice-ministerships, 67.6 percent did not graduate from the First. Similarly, among ambassadors and ministers, a majority came from schools other than the First. An important limiting factor is the fact that there were never enough First Higher School graduates to monopolize positions in the higher civil service.

However, even this weak statistical association between higher school background and position level must be interpreted in context. It is extraordinary to find that 23.3 percent (Level III and above) or 16.8 percent (Level IV and above) of key civil service personnel in a bureaucracy attended a single higher school.[5] It is also noteworthy that in 1954 and 1959 the proportion of First graduates increased at higher levels, and that two out of every five Japanese diplomats attended the First Higher School. There is little doubt that a graduation certificate from the First Higher School carried special honor and prestige. It may also have conferred some competitive advantage in appointment among candidates with similar grades in the civil service examinations, and in promotion among those with similar performance records.

UNIVERSITY

In the prewar Japanese educational system, it was the function of higher schools to provide students with a broad cultural back-

[5] Graduates of Eton, Harrow, or Rugby never accounted for more than 6 per cent respectively in any level or year in the British bureaucracy. Kelsall, *op.cit.*, pp. 122-123.

ground, and the function of universities to equip them with specialized skill and knowledge. At the university level, prospective bureaucrats usually concentrated on the subjects which dominated the prewar higher civil service examinations: law, political science, and economics. Until 1918 only government schools were legally recognized as universities.[6] There were two types of higher institutions: the imperial universities (*teikoku daigaku*) and the "single-course universities" (*tanka daigaku*)—i.e., colleges. By 1918, there were five imperial universities: Tokyo, Kyōto, Tōhoku (at Sendai), Kyūshū (at Fukuoka), and Hokkaidō (at Sapporo).[7] Four others established later had little impact on the higher civil service. Two were in the colonies—Keijō (Seoul) and Taihoku (Taipei), established in 1924 and 1928 respectively, while the other two—Ōsaka (1931) and Nagoya (1939)—did not offer the courses needed for the higher civil service examinations for most of the prewar period.

Among numerous government colleges (*tanka daigaku*), the only one producing a significant number of candidates for the higher civil service was the Tokyo University of Commerce (Tokyo Shōka Daigaku), predecessor of Hitotsubashi University. However, private schools—especially private law schools—produced a large number of applicants for the higher civil service examinations. In 1918, when the University Ordinance (*Daigaku Rei*) was enacted, many of these were given full legal equality with government universities.[8] The most prominent were Waseda, Chūō,

[6] From 1903 to 1918, the government officially sanctioned the use of the name "university" (*daigaku*) by certain private schools but denied them equal status with government universities.

[7] After World War II, the word "*teikoku*" (imperial) was deleted from the names of these universities.

[8] Although Keiō University is popularly regarded as the oldest university in Japan, it was not recognized as a university (with *teikoku daigaku* privileges) until 1920.

Meiji, Keiō, Hōsei, Nihon, and Senshū Universities, of which all except Keiō began primarily as law schools.

Table 20 shows a distribution of the university background of the postwar higher civil servants in this study. Nearly all graduated from the universities they attended, except for some in the Foreign Affairs Ministry who left school as soon as they passed the diplomatic examination. For the few who were able to pass this examination, a university diploma was not considered essential; the ministry was more interested in high scores on the examination and subsequent training in overseas legations and consulates prior to appointments as attaché or élève-consul.

A remarkable feature of Table 20 is the overwhelming ma-

TABLE 20: DISTRIBUTION OF HIGHER CIVIL SERVANTS,
BY UNIVERSITY BACKGROUND

Universities Attended	Proportion	Total
Principal State Universities:		
Tokyo Imperial University	79.0%	
Kyōto Imperial University	5.5%	
Tōhoku Imperial University (Sendai)	3.0%	
The Tokyo University of Commerce	2.0%	
Kyūshū Imperial University (Fukuoka)	1.5%	
Hokkaidō Imperial University	1.4%	
Subtotal:		92.4%
Principal Private Universities:		
Waseda University (Tokyo)	1.0%	
Chūō University (Tokyo)	0.5%	
Meiji University (Tokyo)	0.5%	
Keiō University (Tokyo)	0.4%	
Subtotal:		2.4%
All Other Universities and Colleges	4.0%	
Subtotal:		4.0%
No College Attendance	1.2%	
Subtotal:		1.2%
Total		100.0%

(N = 810; Levels I, II, and III; Core only)

69

jority of the 1949-1959 higher civil servants who came from government universities. Nearly 80 percent attended (and in most instances graduated from) Tokyo Imperial University, while five other government universities supplied another 13 percent. The total attendance at the government universities, therefore, exceeded 92 percent, while the four major private universities accounted for less than 3 percent. Other universities and colleges, such as military academies, agricultural, commercial and technical colleges, and foreign universities, produced only 4 percent. A majority of these came from government technical and vocational higher schools (*senmon gakkō*). Of 1.2 percent who did not attend any college, a few completed only the elementary school level, and some graduated only from middle schools or from the training institutes (*kōshūjo*) of various ministries.

Among the government schools, Tokyo Imperial University has been by far the most important source of postwar higher civil servants. By any standard the proportion of 79.0 percent (Level III and above) represents an extraordinary degree of concentration.[9] Nothing comparable has been found for any other major

[9] Unlike higher schools, universities varied considerably in enrollment. The very size of Tokyo Imperial University facilitated the dominance of its graduates in the higher civil service. However, it was certainly not the only factor, for other universities did not produce higher civil servants in proportion to their size. The following are the numbers of graduates of major universities in 1935:

Tokyo Imperial University	2,276
Kyōto Imperial University	1,451
Tōhoku Imperial University	441
The Tokyo University of Commerce	639
Kyūshū Imperial University	553
Hokkaidō Imperial University	644
Waseda University	2,747
Chūō University	840
Meiji University	1,145
Keiō University	1,977

From the Ministry of Education, comp., *op.cit.*, pp. 180, 267, 281.

nation. In the U.S. federal government, for instance, the largest group among the 1940 higher civil servants were Harvard graduates, with Georgetown graduates second, but these groups accounted for only 11.2 percent and 6.9 percent respectively.[10] However, another study based upon a different sample shows that the largest group (four-year degrees) among the 1959 federal career civil service executives came from George Washington University, and that its proportion was only 3 percent.[11] In the British bureaucracy, where university background has traditionally been more important, Oxford and Cambridge graduates in 1950 constituted 26.5 percent and 20.8 percent respectively of all higher civil servants with the rank of assistant secretary or above.[12] Even the combined total for these two famous universities (47.3 percent) is far below the proportion for Tokyo Imperial University (79.0 percent) alone.

The Japanese case is perhaps even more significant in terms of quality than of quantity. The impact of education on values and attitudes is probably greater in Japan than in many other nations because the Japanese people show smaller differences in such qualities as ethnic origin, religion, language, and regionalism, which in other nations profoundly influence the process of socialization. The prewar Japanese educational system was highly stratified and centralized, and at its apex stood Tokyo Imperial University. This attracted the most brilliant students in the country regardless of regional or social origin, and gave them a common experience and training. In this sense the intellectual quality as well as the degree of homogeneity of the Japanese higher bureaucracy was extraordinarily high. Thus in their common background at Tokyo Imperial University we find one of the most important sources of both the cohesiveness and the potential strength and effectiveness of this remarkable body of bureaucrats.

[10] Bendix, *op.cit.*, p. 92. [11] Warner et al., *op.cit.*, p. 373.
[12] Kelsall, *op.cit.*, p. 136.

4 · EDUCATIONAL BACKGROUNDS

Having established this striking concentration of Tokyo Imperial University graduates at the higher levels, we need to ascertain their specific locations within the postwar bureaucracy. Table 21 presents a distribution by ministry of graduates of Tokyo Imperial University among the 1949-1959 higher civil servants. Unlike First Higher School graduates, Tokyo Imperial University graduates are predominant in every ministry in the core or periphery,

TABLE 21: PROPORTION OF HIGHER CIVIL SERVANTS WHO ATTENDED TOKYO IMPERIAL UNIVERSITY, BY MINISTRY

Core	Proportion	Proportion	Periphery
Education	95.7%		
		89.3%	Board of Audit
Finance	89.0%		
International Trade and Industry	86.6%		
Economic Stabilization Board	86.2%		
Justice	85.7%		
		85.2%	Imperial Household Agency
Transportation	84.3%		
Agriculture and Forestry	80.7%		
Foreign Affairs	79.3%		
Prime Minister's Office	76.5%		
Postal Services	73.3%		
		70.2%	Ambassadors and Ministers
Construction	64.3%		
Welfare	63.3%		
		60.6%	National Personnel Authority
Labor	57.1%		
Telecommunications	42.9%		
Total (Core only)	79.0%		

(N = 1,002; Levels I, II, III and diplomats)

and form a majority in every ministry except Telecommunications.[13] However, the specific proportion varies substantially from one ministry to another, the smallest being 42.9 percent and the largest 95.7 percent. The pattern resembles that for First Higher School graduates, for the relative prestige of ministries and promotion patterns are related to this variation. For example, Finance, International Trade and Industry, and the Economic Stabilization Board tended to recruit large numbers of Tokyo Imperial University graduates, and these graduates eventually occupied an overwhelming proportion of higher civil service positions. But it was also generally true that once they entered any ministry, Tokyo graduates tended to be promoted more rapidly than graduates of other schools. They even dominated the higher levels of such ministries as Education or the Board of Audit, even though these were not especially prestigious.

Certain deviations in Table 21 require explanation. First, the proportion for the National Personnel Authority (60.6 percent) is somewhat lower than the average in the core (79.0 percent). This was due in part to a deliberate policy which this organization was supposed to apply throughout the government, i.e., equality in personnel administration regardless of educational background.[14] Obviously this policy, while more honored in the National Personnel Authority than elsewhere in the government, was scarcely an unqualified success even there. Second, the proportion of Tokyo University graduates among diplomats is unexpectedly low, although the proportion of First Higher School graduates among them is higher than usual. One reason is that an appreciable

---

[13] Although the proportion in Telecommunications was less than 50.0 percent, no other university supplied even close to 42.9 percent of the higher officials in this ministry.

[14] For instance, no two personnel officers (*jinji kan*) can be graduates of the same faculty of the same university; the National Public Service Law, Article 5, par. 5.

proportion (13.4 percent) were graduates of the Tokyo University of Commerce. A highly clustered distribution of graduates of this university affects the figures for some other core ministries as well. Although they accounted for only a small part of the total number of higher civil servants (2.0 percent in Level III or above), they were concentrated in such important ministries as Finance, Foreign Affairs, and International Trade and Industry. Accordingly, the proportions of Tokyo University graduates for these ministries are somewhat lower than they would otherwise be.

Another important question concerning university background is its relation to position level. Table 22 displays the distribution of Tokyo Imperial University graduates by survey year and position level.

TABLE 22: PROPORTION OF HIGHER CIVIL SERVANTS WHO ATTENDED TOKYO IMPERIAL UNIVERSITY, BY YEAR AND LEVEL

| Year | Level | | | | Total |
	I	II	III	IV	
1949	58.7%	80.7%	67.8%	64.0%	65.8%
1954	89.7%	80.5%	82.6%	69.8%	72.7%
1959	95.0%	85.8%	72.7%	63.1%	68.5%
Total	80.0%	82.7%	73.8%	65.7%	68.9%

(N = 1,090; Core only)

By and large, Table 22 exhibits a pattern similar to that of higher school background (Table 19) in the sense that position level is generally correlated with educational background. The two deviating features—an unusually small figure for 1949 Level I and a reversal of the order between Levels II and III in 1954 or 1959—also appear in this table. In some respects, however, Table 22 differs significantly from Table 19: the association between position level and university background is markedly stronger owing to the overall increase in proportion, and among the 1959 group, the correlation reaches almost an ideal degree.[15]

The relationship between Levels II and III can be understood in terms of the historical structure of the Japanese bureaucracy. Levels I, II, and IV have been the standard echelons throughout the upper bureaucracy, whereas Level III has existed only in part of the bureaucracy and tends to be specialized in function. After 1945, the number of Level III positions (chiefs of division and assistant chiefs of division) expanded considerably, and their function became less specialized than before. By 1959, however, many of the new divisions had been upgraded to bureaus. It is partly a reflection of these changes that in Table 22 the Level III proportion was higher than the Level II proportion in 1954 but lower in 1949 and 1959. Also, Levels II and III belonged to the same general pay category,[16] so that in many tables in the present study, differences between these levels are minor.

A more conspicuous deviation is seen in 1949 Level I. The reasons for this unusually low proportion of Tokyo University graduates here are the same as in Table 19. First, the effect of the Allied Occupation's purges was greater in Level I than at lower levels, both in actual dismissals and in voluntary resignations prompted by fear of dismissal. It was natural that the highest echelons of the bureaucracy were most affected by the great political change resulting from the termination of World War II. The purge began in January 1946, and reached its peak in 1947 and 1948. De-purging on a significant scale began in October 1950, and was completed by the time the peace treaty became effective in 1952.[17]

---

[15] As explained in Chapter 2, the proportion for the highest level (I) must approach 100.0 percent in order to substantiate the maximum degree of correlation. The proportion for the lowest level (IV), however, cannot be expected to be 0.0 per cent in data concerning promotion.

[16] The National Personnel Authority Rule, Article 9-8.

[17] Hans H. Baerwald, *The Purge of Japanese Leaders under the Occupation* (Berkeley: University of California Press, 1959), pp. 78-79; Sōri Fu

Second, the 1949 figure reflects, in addition to the exodus of key officials, American efforts to encourage the promotion of graduates of other universities. The Hoover Mission, which visited Japan from November 1946 to June 1947, criticized the "excessive" concentration of Tokyo Imperial University graduates in the higher civil service.[18] The Allied Occupation ended in April 1952, and as Table 22 shows, the distribution returned to a "normal" pattern by 1954, or certainly by 1959.

Although the impact of the Allied Occupation upon the bureaucracy was profound, it was by no means revolutionary. Efforts to reform the bureaucracy were considerably hampered by the necessity of using the existing bureaucracy to administer other programs for the democratization of Japan.[19] According to the one source, only 11.9 percent of the "higher civil service personnel" were removed in the initial purge, and 60.0 percent of these were in the Home Ministry (*Naimu Shō*).[20] Recent studies of the purge conclude that it had only a minor effect upon the civil service.[21] So far as education is concerned, our data support this conclusion. The impact was largely limited to Level I, while at other levels deviation, if any, tends to be very small in Table 22 or any other

---

Kambō Kansa Ka, comp., *Kōshoku tsuihō ni kansuru oboegaki gaitōsha meibo* (Tokyo: Hibiya Seikeikai, 1949), "Kōshoku tsuihō jimu no keika," pp. 1-14.

[18] Blaine Hoover, Malino F. DeAngelis, Robert S. Hare, and W. Pierce MacCoy, *Report of the United States Personnel Advisory Mission to Japan, Submitted to the Supreme Commander of the Allied Powers* (unpublished, June 1947), pp. 13-15.

[19] Supreme Commander for the Allied Powers, General Headquarters, *History of Nonmilitary Activities of the Occupation of Japan, 1945-1951* (unpublished, 1951), Vol. 5, Pt. 6, pp. 23-24.

[20] *Ibid.*, pp. 26-27. Although the definition of "higher civil service personnel" is not clear, they appear to be *chokunin* officials or an equivalent group.

[21] Baerwald, *op.cit.*, pp. 82-83; John D. Montgomery, *Forced to Be Free* (Chicago: University of Chicago Press, 1957), pp. 86-89.

table in this study. Furthermore, the limited impact of the American reform efforts is also seen within Level I itself. Among those with the very highest rank (administrative vice-ministers) in the 1949-1959 period, 83.8 percent were Tokyo Imperial University graduates, while the remainder were Kyōto Imperial University graduates (16.2 percent). In other words, in 1949 or in any other survey year, only graduates of the two most prominent universities were serving in the highest civil service positions.

FIELD OF ACADEMIC SPECIALIZATION

It may well be argued that what higher civil servants study is more important than what school they attend. But even in this respect, the Japanese bureaucracy shows unusual homogeneity. At the upper levels, the administrative machinery is dominated by men trained in law, since the prewar higher civil service examinations consisted largely of subjects taught only or primarily at the faculties of law (*hōgaku bu*) at Japanese universities. It is essential, however, to realize that Japanese faculties of law are quite different from American law schools in curriculum and objective.

Structural and curricular variations from one university to another were minimized by government regulations binding on private as well as on public universities. Standardization was also fostered by the uniform higher civil service examinations. The principal subjects in the examinations were law, political science, and economics, which were chiefly taught at faculties of law. After World War I, Tokyo and Kyōto Imperial Universities carved separate Faculties of Economics out of their Faculties of Law. But the two faculties remained closely associated, and students in one generally took courses in the other. In other schools, the two fields remained within the same faculty as sections(*ka*). Political science and law were even more firmly linked. At Tokyo Imperial University, as in most other universities, these two sections were always

77

placed within the Faculty of Law, and students specializing in one section were required to take courses in the other.

In short, the training of men for the private practice of law was only one function of a Japanese faculty of law, and very often not the primary function at all. Many students had no desire to become attorneys. They entered faculties of law to acquire general managerial skill. Although faculties of law in fact offered few courses specifically concerned with management, accounting, or personnel administration, it was generally understood that faculties of law were providing a "broad" background for managerial skill. Japanese industry, banking, shipping, and commerce preferred law graduates for managerial positions as did the bureaucracy. In terms of objective, therefore, a Japanese faculty of law more nearly resembled a combination of a political science department and a business administration school in an American university than it did a law school. Private attorneys and judges came chiefly from the legal sections of law faculties,[22] but the managerial personnel of private business and higher civil service came almost equally from both the legal and the political science sections, which in substance were rather similar.

Inclusion of political science, and often of economics as well, in a faculty of law meant that the faculty of letters in a Japanese university was without these subjects. On the other hand, the faculty of letters, despite its title, taught not only the humanities but also the other social sciences. Thus sociology, psychology, and anthropology were sections of the faculty of letters. While a liberal arts college in the United States is considered a "general-purpose" institution and a law school a "special-purpose" institution, a Japanese faculty of letters tends to be "special-purpose" and a Japanese faculty of law "general-purpose" in terms of training and purpose.

[22] After passing the judicial section of the higher civil service examinations, they sometimes received additional training at courts, procuratorial bureaus or a special institute.

Many graduates of faculties of letters entered only the specific fields for which they were trained in universities, and the remainder became teachers. Law graduates, however, entered nearly every field, and even some literary fields such as journalism were dominated by law graduates.

Tables 23, 24, and 25 deal with the fields of academic specialization of the 1949-1959 higher civil servants. Table 23 shows a distribution of the faculties which they attended. Separate figures are given for the two sections of law and political science. However, it must be emphasized again that the curricula of the two were much more similar than their names implied, and that they overlapped at many points. Furthermore, the bureaucracy and the corporations saw little difference between graduates of these two sections for recruitment or promotion purposes. More than half of the cases attended the legal sections and more than one-sixth attended the political science sections of various universities. In the aggregate, more than two-thirds of postwar higher civil servants at Level III and above were supplied by faculties of law.

TABLE 23: Distribution of Higher Civil Servants, by Field of Academic Specialization

Faculty		Proportion
Law: Legal Section	50.4%	
Political Science Section	18.1%	68.5%
Engineering		12.2%
Economics		5.4%
Agriculture		4.8%
Natural Sciences		1.9%
Literature		0.8%
Others		3.2%
Unknown*		3.2%
Total		100.0%

(N = 810; Levels I, II, and III; Core only)
* Includes those who did not attend college.

79

The dominance of law graduates, of course, left only minor shares for the graduates of other faculties. However, it is significant to note that engineering faculties exceeded economics faculties in the production of higher officials, although economics faculties were more often mentioned as a promising background in memoirs and other literature. The proportion for agriculture, though small, is greater than that for natural sciences or literature. Although the fact is difficult to determine on the basis of our data, most nonlaw and noneconomics graduates apparently did not go through the prewar normal course of the higher civil service examinations. Their promotion pattern was, as will be discussed in Chapter 5, different from that of law or economics graduates.

At any rate, the most remarkable feature of Table 23 is the overwhelming proportion of law graduates. This feature is especially striking to American observers, and was perhaps the aspect that most disturbed the members of the Hoover Mission. With their educational backgrounds in mind, the Hoover Report charged that most higher civil servants were "unqualified" for their positions and that the higher bureaucracy of Japan remained essentially "feudal."[23] The Occupation's attempts to reform the Japanese bureaucracy, as embodied in the National Public Service Law of 1948, reflected this charge,[24] and attempted to place specialists rather than generalists (i.e., law graduates) in higher civil service positions. It is, however, clear from our 1954 and 1959 data that the attempt did not enjoy much long-range success.

It has been mentioned that the Japanese faculty of law was a general-purpose institution whose graduates entered nearly every occupational field. Such educational policy and recruitment practice are clearly reflected in Table 24, which lists the proportion of law graduates for each ministry. Whether a ministry was concerned with fiscal matters (Finance, the Economic Stabilization Board, or

[23] Hoover et al., *op.cit.*, pp. 13-15.
[24] The law has since been substantially amended.

the Board of Audit), diplomacy (Foreign Affairs or diplomats), learning (Education), or social or economic welfare (Labor and Welfare), it was dominated by higher civil servants who had attended faculties of law. In all except two ministries, more than half the higher administrators were trained in law. It was inevitable for Occupation officials to conclude that most Japanese higher civil servants were "unqualified" for the positions that they held. Whether his charge has merit will be discussed later in this chapter and also in Chapter 5.

TABLE 24: PROPORTION OF HIGHER CIVIL SERVANTS WHO STUDIED LAW OR POLITICAL SCIENCE, BY MINISTRY

Core	Proportion	Proportion	Periphery
Justice	92.1%		
		85.7%	Board of Audit
		81.5%	Imperial Household Agency
Foreign Affairs	79.3%		
Finance	78.0%		
Postal Services	77.8%		
Economic Stabilization Board	75.9%		
Education	73.9%		
Prime Minister's Office	72.4%		
		72.3%	Ambassadors and Ministers
Labor	66.7%		
Transportation	65.7%		
International Trade and Industry	63.9%		
		60.6%	National Personnel Authority
Welfare	57.1%		
Agriculture and Forestry	54.2%		
Construction	46.4%		
Telecommunications	23.8%		
Total (Core only)	68.5%		

(N = 1,002; Levels I, II, III and diplomats)

Although so high a proportion of law graduates is remarkable, it varies considerably from one ministry to another. Some of the reasons for such a variation are readily identifiable. The proportion is understandably highest in the Justice Ministry, where legal training is functionally imperative. Key positions in this ministry are by convention held almost entirely by public procurators who have passed the judicial examinations. (However, not many former justices held posts in the Justice Ministry.) The proportions also tend to be high in the economic ministries (Finance, the Economic Stabilization Board, International Trade and Industry). The total proportion of economics graduates reaching the higher levels was so small (5.4 percent) that these ministries were bound to be, by the traditional bias, dominated by law graduates. Even councillors (*shingikan*) to the Economic Planning Agency were mostly law graduates during the 1949-1959 period.

In some ministries, the proportion of law graduates is relatively low. In Agriculture and Forestry, the percentage is reduced by a sizable group who attended faculties of agriculture; in Construction and Telecommunications the percentages are reduced by large groups of engineering graduates. In these ministries men with specialist educations more often reached higher positions than in other ministries. Yet the proportions trained in law were always large, and the higher ranks of nearly every ministry were staffed by a majority of generalists (law graduates) and a varying but generally small portion of specialists.

There has been a widespread belief in the Japanese bureaucracy, in the business world, and in higher education that the generalist is by and large superior to the specialist in filling supervisory posts. The Board of Audit, for instance, seldom had professional accountants or auditors in its higher administrative positions. Key positions in the Education Ministry were not necessarily held by former educators. This, of course, did not mean that the bureaucracy lacked persons who were especially trained and qualified for specific tasks; they usually held part-time consultative positions or inferior supervisory positions. Without such specialists, the bureaucracy could not have maintained satisfactory levels of performance. Highly specialized persons, however, were usually excluded from senior supervisory positions.

Such a philosophy of personnel administration is generally corroborated by Table 25, which shows a distribution of law or political science graduates by position level. The low proportion in 1949 Level I is caused by the same factors that have already been mentioned with respect to Table 22, while the very low proportion for 1949 Level III is apparently a result of American efforts to place specialists in these relatively high positions. However, in the 1954 and 1959 data, position level and legal education are clearly correlated, demonstrating the superior position of generalists. Although not as high as the relationship between university and position level in 1959 (Table 22), the degree of association for legal education in 1954 and 1959 is considerable.

TABLE 25: PROPORTION OF HIGHER CIVIL SERVANTS WHO STUDIED LAW OR POLITICAL SCIENCE, BY YEAR AND LEVEL

Year	I	II	III	IV	Total
1949	60.9%	73.7%	49.2%	53.0%	54.9%
1954	89.4%	73.7%	64.1%	56.3%	59.9%
1959	82.5%	74.2%	63.6%	60.7%	63.8%
Total	76.8%	73.9%	58.1%	56.4%	59.4%

(N = 1,090; Core only)

It might be expected that a bureaucracy of this sort would seem unsatisfactory to American specialists in personnel administration, for whom a high degree of functional specialization is fundamental to a modern bureaucracy.[25] Many Japanese critics also have long complained of the "omnipotence of legal studies" (*hōka bannō*), meaning this type of preference for law graduates in appointment and promotion.[26] It appears, however, that Japanese critics are concerned not so much with specialization and efficiency as with the fact that an "excessive" share of senior (thus high-paying) posts were held by one group (generalists) at the cost of the other (specialists). At any rate, despite American efforts and domestic criticisms, the "omnipotence of legal studies" has so far remained largely invincible.

Law graduates, however, are not lawyers in the ordinary sense of the term. They are not members of the bar, and unless they go into the Justice Ministry, they rarely study practical cases. The difference between the curricula of the Japanese law faculty and the American law school has already been mentioned. In addition, it must not be forgotten that before law graduates reach supervisory positions at Level IV or above, they have normally spent ten years or more in lower positions in the same ministry or some other ministries. They are thus far from being as ignorant of the ministry's specialized function as critics like to imply. Merely by reviewing the performance of the bureaucracy in agriculture, industrialization, or education, it is difficult to conclude that key civil servants were in any generic sense unqualified for their task. Particularly in the economic sphere, the achievement of postwar bureaucrats has been impressive, even though most of them were law graduates. Officials of the Budget Bureau and the Economic Planning Agency have been critically involved in drafting the annual budgets and formulating the long-range economic policies

[25] In the U.S. higher civil service, the proportion of law school graduates is generally very low. Kilpatrick et al., *op.cit.* (IPCR), reports that it was 9.9 per cent in 1960.

[26] See, for example, Nihon Hyōronsha, ed., *Nihon no hōgaku: Kaiko to tembō* (Tokyo: Nihon Hyōronsha, 1950), pp. 266-267. This book contains a discussion of legal education by leading educators in Japan.

that undoubtedly influenced the remarkable postwar recovery and expansion of the Japanese economy.

Use of law graduates as supervisors of specialists may well increase the number of personnel required, and may also discourage innovation in some fields. However, it also makes Japanese higher civil servants a very homogeneous group, strongly infused with elitism. Being a graduate of the Faculty of Law of Tokyo University carries special weight in the bureaucracy, in business, and in many other fields in Japan, and creates keen awareness of elite status. Of postwar higher civil servants, 68.5 percent were graduates of faculties of law (see Table 23), but more significantly 66.4 percent were graduates of the Faculty of Law of Tokyo Imperial University. So homogeneous a group inevitably acquires elitist status within the bureaucracy, and is capable of exerting enormous power.

SCHOOL CLIQUES

Tables 20 through 25 leave little doubt that the Japanese higher civil service, even in the postwar period, has been dominated by graduates of Tokyo Imperial University, especially those of its Faculty of Law. Criticism of the dominant position of law graduates in the upper bureaucracy has been more than matched by criticism of the dominant position of Tokyo University graduates. In particular, it has been said that appointment or promotion depended upon favoritism based upon the school attended, and that key positions were monopolized by members of a few exclusive school cliques or *gakubatsu*.

The term *gakubatsu* implies clannishness among graduates of the same school and discrimination against graduates of other schools, especially in appointment and promotion. Even if there were no evidence of such cliques, the widespread popular belief in their existence would make *gakubatsu* a significant factor in studying the bureaucracy. There is, of course, a considerable body

85

of evidence that *gakubatsu* do exist as informal, sometimes almost unconscious, associations of men with the same school background. The difficulty lies in determining the nature and the importance of such associations, and in drawing causal inferences. Do men succeed in the civil service merely because they attend certain prominent schools, or do so many bright students prefer these schools that their graduates are predestined to a higher rate of achievement in the bureaucracy?

The ties referred to by critics of *gakubatsu* vary with the particular educational backgrounds of the critics. Those who are not graduates of Tokyo University, and especially those who are from private universities, usually employ the term *gakubatsu* to mean a Tokyo University clique. Partly as a defense mechanism and partly from subjective experience, Tokyo University graduates often argue that their number is so large in the bureaucracy that association depends more upon a common higher school background than upon a common university experience. Some critics thus narrow the denotation of *gakubatsu* to mean primarily Tokyo University graduates who came from the First Higher School, and secondarily several other similar cliques based on different higher school backgrounds.

The popular emphasis on the importance of higher school ties in explaining social relations has, if anything, increased since these schools were abolished in 1949-1951 and replaced by *high schools* (similar to American high schools), operating at lower age levels and with different educational objectives. Nostalgia is clearly a factor in this emphasis. The prewar higher school entrance examination was considered the most difficult hurdle for students aspiring to enter the imperial universities. Once this was surmounted, the pressures relaxed a bit. Partly for this reason and partly because of the nature of the curriculum, many students found higher school life easier and more carefree than either their earlier life or uni-

86

versity life. At least, they often behaved as if they were free from "earthly" matters and "trivial" concerns in higher schools.

Evidence of this can be found not only in numerous memoirs and biographies but also in commemorative anthologies dedicated to higher school professors.[27] Pleasant memories of higher school, combined with association at earlier ages and in smaller groups than in universities, and the more personal character of instruction tended to establish strong ties of friendship among higher school students. In particular, because of their ages and the extreme selectivity in admission to these schools, higher school students were often imbued with elitist sentiments. It is perhaps also significant that the alumni associations of prewar higher schools and their publications, especially those of the numbered schools, survive despite the disappearance of the schools themselves.

The data presented in this chapter, however, make it difficult to explain *gakubatsu* solely in terms of higher school background. The largest group of higher school graduates among the postwar higher civil servants surveyed came from the First Higher School, which accounted for 23.3 percent of the total in Level III and above. In one organization the proportion reached 53.6 percent (the Board of Audit), but on the whole the correlation between First Higher School background and position level was slight, and little evidence was found that a particular higher school background was "essential" in reaching the highest positions in the civil service.

Two factors in particular may have limited the significance of higher school ties among higher administrators. First, the small size of graduating classes in higher schools insured that no single

[27] See, for instance, Maeda Tamon and Takagi Yasaka, eds., *Nitobe hakushi tsuioku shū* (Tokyo: Ko Nitobe Hakushi Kinen Jigyō Jikkō Iinkai, 1936). Few educators in Japan have exerted as much influence among state university students as Dr. Nitobe Inazō. Many contributors to this volume were higher civil servants.

school, not even the First, could monopolize key positions in the bureaucracy or any other field. At the same time, the very smallness of such a group tended to make school tie favoritism conspicuous in the bureaucracy, thus tending to alienate others and to work against the interests of those in that group. Second, the farther a graduate moved in time from his higher school, the more likely he was to undergo a variety of experiences, to acquire new interests, to find new friends, and to associate with persons other than his higher school classmates, regardless of his attachment to the old school. It thus became not only more difficult but also less practical to stress his higher school background and to maintain strong higher school ties as he advanced up the social and bureaucratic ladders. Memories of higher school might remain as a source of warm personal relationships and perpetuate alumni gatherings. Higher school ties might be strong in a microscopic sense, but in a macroscopic sense they tended to be more sentimental and symbolic than practical or political.

Our data on university background differ from those on higher school background in at least one respect. They show a more pronounced concentration of graduates from a single institution. While First Higher School graduates constituted only about one-fourth of higher civil servants at Level III and above, Tokyo Imperial University graduates accounted for nearly four-fifths at Level III and above. Moreover, the promotion pattern within the higher civil service was more explicitly related to university background than to higher school background. Although the promotion pattern will be more intensively examined in the next chapter, it is indisputable that Tokyo University graduates dominated the upper echelons of the postwar bureaucracy.

Prewar universities, as indicated previously, probably provided a less emotional and more superficial basis for association than higher schools, and university ties were somewhat less likely to develop into intimate personal relationships after graduation. On the other hand, university education, especially that of the Faculty of Law of Tokyo University, was directly related to career goals and professional advancement and undoubtedly gave rise to common interests. Graduation from Tokyo Imperial University has always carried very high prestige in modern Japan regardless of higher school background or record. It may be concluded, therefore, that attending this university was an important factor in the social and professional status hierarchy. Its graduates shared not only a common experience but also common interests, and formed a loosely knit group possessed of considerable prominence and power.

Originally, the predominance of Tokyo University graduates in higher civil service positions was a result of lack of competition, since this was the first and, for a considerable period, the only university in Japan. As competition increased with the steady expansion of the school system, Tokyo graduates began to acquire a vested interest in protecting their favored position in the higher civil service. In this manner their university ties became a matter of controversy, especially for those attempting to "intrude" into the "exclusive club." Moreover, the fact that they were so numerous in the government made ingroup favoritism not only probable but also less provable, since there were always many Tokyo University graduates who did not rise as fast as others.

Even so, it would be inappropriate to overemphasize the significance of common university background. Critics of *gakubatsu* often assume, consciously or unconsciously, that all Tokyo University graduates shared identical attitudes and values. This is a proposition which cannot be reconciled with human psychology or empirical evidence. The Faculty of Law produced communists as well as capitalists, liberal democrats as well as ultranationalists, and there were wide variations in outlook among its professors as well as its students. Recruitment into the civil service somewhat narrowed such variations but it by no means completely eliminated them. Numerous memoirs and records make it abundantly clear that considerable diversity remained among those Tokyo University graduates who reached high positions in the bureaucracy.

Nor can we accept a literal interpretation of *gakubatsu*. Most members of a graduating class of Tokyo Imperial University probably did not associate with each other beyond recognizing their existence as a class. Close relationships were limited to small circles. Even in higher schools, which were much smaller, it is doubtful that really meaningful associations extended as far as to an entire graduating class. The forces which have sustained *gakubatsu* are not basically friendships cultivated at higher school or university but more impersonal relationships based on a sense of mutual advantage as well as upon the honor and prestige of the university attended. The case of Tokyo University graduates provides the best single example of this phenomenon. It is clearly a more important factor in explaining *gakubatsu* than higher schools.

Extensive though it may be, favoritism based on school ties is probably practiced more subtly than our statistics imply. In a state as modern as Japan, a higher administrator is unlikely to choose his subordinates solely on the basis of school background and without regard for competence. He may be swayed by school ties in choosing among men who appear equally qualified for a position. Potential ability is, of course, difficult to measure precisely, and it is on these grounds that the critics of the Tokyo University clique are vulnerable to counterattack. The enormous prestige accorded Tokyo University could scarcely have survived without some basis other than past glory. Its reputation made it the first choice of the ablest students throughout the nation. Particularly since 1893 when the administrative higher civil service examinations were required of applicants from all universities, critics have been hard pressed to demonstrate that Tokyo Imperial University graduates were advancing not by merit but by favoritism. Each year many Tokyo University graduates failed the examinations; yet those who passed always far outnumbered the successful candidates from other universities.

Finally, it should be noted that the role of "school cliques" varies from one organizational setting to another. It is perhaps strongest and most salient in the bureaucracy and in the academic world, less notable in commerce and industry, and still less important in politics, especially in left-wing movements. Similarly, school ties are less meaningful in relations among organizations than within a particular organization. Especially when the interests of two organizations come into conflict, the outcome is not apt to be influenced by *gakubatsu* ties. This is evident not only in business but also in government, where occupational ties and practical interests are sometimes far more important than university ties. One often hears, for instance, of a "Foreign Ministry clique" or—even after the abolition of the Home Ministry (*Naimu Shō*)—of a "Home Ministry clique." These represent cases where school-based ties are overlaid, and often replaced, by patterns of association based on common professional and career experiences and interests.

CHAPTER 5

Career Patterns

NONBUREAUCRATIC CAREERS

HAVING analyzed the origins and educational backgrounds of higher civil servants, we now turn to an examination of patterns in their bureaucratic careers. A major characteristic of the 1949-1959 higher civil servants is that most of them entered the government soon after graduating from universities and remained in the service for about twenty years. The concept of career service in Japan is strong not only in the bureaucracy but also in industry, commerce, and higher education. Men expect, and are expected, to stay with the same organization until retirement. Furthermore, seniority is considered so critical in promotion that the range of labor mobility, especially at managerial levels, is traditionally very narrow.

Table 26 sets forth the proportion of postwar higher civil servants who worked elsewhere either before entering the service or during interruptions in their civil service careers. The figures in the total row indicate that approximately 9 percent held full-time non-bureaucratic jobs before beginning their bureaucratic careers, and that about 3 percent interrupted their government careers at some point prior to retirement to accept outside positions. There were some chronological changes, especially from 1949 to 1954. Those who began careers in fields other than the civil service were more numerous in 1949, evidently because of changes in recruitment and promotion policies under the Allied Occupation. Even in 1949, however, more than 84 percent of higher civil servants had worked only in the government. By and large, mobility was low

5 · CAREER PATTERNS

TABLE 26: Proportion of Higher Civil Servants with
Nonbureaucratic Employment Before or After Entering
the Service, by Year

Year	Proportion with Nonbureaucratic Employment		Proportion Without Nonbureaucratic Employment	Total
	Before Entering	After Entering		
1949	14.0%	1.4%	84.6%	100.0%
1954	6.5%	4.5%	89.0%	100.0%
1959	5.3%	3.8%	90.0%	100.0%
Total	8.8%	3.1%	88.1%	100.0%

(N = 805; Levels I, II, and III; Core only)

during the survey period; only about one in ten higher administrators had held nonbureaucratic positions.

When the same data are tabulated in a different manner, however, nonbureaucratic careers exhibit a good deal of variation. Table 27 shows the distribution by ministry of those who had not held nonbureaucratic occupations before the survey years (or had always remained in the civil service). Some prestigious ministries rank high in the list. The proportions for Finance, International Trade and Industry, and Foreign Affairs are remarkably high, showing the strong tendency of these administrators to think in terms of a life career in the government. On the other hand, the proportion for the Economic Stabilization Board is unexpectedly low. It is clear that the distribution in Table 27 is related not only to prestige but also to special circumstances or customs in the Japanese bureaucracy. The figure for the Economic Stabilization Board reflects the immediate postwar policy of recruiting experienced individuals from private business to aid in restoring the national economy.

Similarly, the proportions are fairly low for Labor, the Prime Minister's Office, and Justice. The newly created Labor Ministry usually recruited a few social critics or journalists for important

93

TABLE 27: PROPORTION OF HIGHER CIVIL SERVANTS WITHOUT
NONBUREAUCRATIC EMPLOYMENT, BY MINISTRY

Core	Proportion	Proportion	Periphery
Finance	97.5%		
Postal Services	95.6%		
International Trade and Industry	93.8%		
Foreign Affairs	93.1%		
Transportation	92.9%		
Construction	92.8%		
Telecommunications	90.5%		
Agriculture and Forestry	90.3%		
Labor	85.7%		
		85.7%	Board of Audit
Economic Stabilization Board	82.8%		
Prime Minister's Office	82.6%		
Justice	82.6%		
Welfare	77.6%		
		76.0%	Ambassadors and Ministers
Education	65.2%		
		54.5%	National Personnel Authority
		48.2%	Imperial Household Agency
Total (Core only)	88.1%		

(N = 997; Levels I, II, III, and diplomats)

positions, and generally appointed a woman to head the Bureau of Women and Minors. Women were not admitted to the prewar higher civil service examinations and very few have entered the higher civil service. In this survey, there are no women except the chief of this bureau and a few chiefs of section in the same bureau. The Justice Ministry sometimes recruited private attorneys for high positions, and the Prime Minister's Office took a variety of experienced men from private business and other fields.

The proportion for Welfare is relatively low, reflecting the use of medical doctors for certain high posts and former military officers for veterans' affairs. The Education Ministry, with by far the highest percentage of higher administrators having outside experience, is a special case. The figure is a result of frequent movement between educational institutions and this ministry.[1] It has not been uncommon for those in the Education Ministry to begin their careers as teachers and eventually to become bureaucrats or to interrupt their bureaucratic careers in order to accept teaching positions. The movement has been largely between government higher schools or universities and the bureaucracy. Those who began in or went to private institutions have seldom become higher administrators. Conversely, the high proportion of those opting for a lifetime career with Postal Services is largely a result of lack of comparable private opportunities. Since few private organizations resembled this ministry in function, the nonbureaucratic mobility of its personnel was generally limited.

In the periphery, the proportions without nonbureaucratic experience are much smaller than in the core. The pattern suggests that the concept of career service was weaker in the periphery than in the core, and that the outlook of peripheral officials was different in many ways. The lowest proportion, less than 50 percent for the Imperial Household Agency, was due to the recruitment of many educators and former aristocrats to this organization. Similarly, higher officials in the National Personnel Authority included former professors, journalists, and social critics.

Although most Japanese diplomats were drawn from the ranks of higher officials in the Foreign Affairs Ministry proper, an appreciable portion of them held nonbureaucratic occupations before or between assignments to diplomatic posts. However, within

[1] Although legally the employees of the national schools have been classified as civil servants, they are not defined as civil servants in this study (see chapter 2).

95

the peripheral organizations, the diplomatic corps made relatively less use of genuine "outsiders" than the others. In the Board of Audit, the proportion without nonbureaucratic experience is highest in the periphery. In this organization the concept of career service was held as rigidly as in the typical core ministry.

The preceding analysis suggests the possibility that the higher the position a bureaucrat held, the more likely he was to have had nonbureaucratic experience. Although the mobility of labor at managerial levels has been generally low in Japan, it has certainly not been nil. Furthermore, it is often thought that this mobility, though small, increases as the level increases. It is not necessarily unusual in Japan that well-known businessmen switch corporations. As shown in Table 27, diplomats tend to have more outside experience than those in the Foreign Affairs Ministry proper. Table 28 presents data on this question.

TABLE 28: Proportion of Higher Civil Servants with Nonbureaucratic Employment, by Year and Level

Year	Level				Total
	I	II	III	IV	
1949	19.6%	8.8%	14.4%	16.2%	15.4%
1954	18.4%	10.2%	8.8%	11.5%	11.3%
1959	17.9%	11.7%	9.2%	8.3%	9.2%
Total	18.7%	10.4%	11.1%	12.2%	12.1%

(N = 1,084; Core only)

The proportion of higher civil servants with nonbureaucratic experience at Level I is markedly higher than at any other level. The proportions for Level I are nearly twice as great as those for Level II. The pattern is persistent through all the survey years and substantiates the recruitment of some distinguished persons at the highest level. Although the rate of mobility may be lower for the Japanese bureaucracy than for other major bureaucracies, it is nonetheless interesting to see that about one out of every five Level I officials had held a nonbureaucratic position either before or after entering the civil service.

An equally significant feature of Table 28 is that there are some noticeable chronological changes in nonbureaucratic experience. In 1949 there was an inverse relationship between nonbureaucratic experience and Levels II, III, and IV. A much weaker association was found for these levels in 1954, but in 1959 the pattern was reversed to a positive relationship. These figures suggest that in addition to substantial recruitment of outside personnel at the highest level, in 1949 appreciable outside recruitment apparently took place for the positions of chiefs of division and chiefs of section. While the impact of the Allied Occupation was most clearly felt at Level I, as shown in the data on university background (Table 22), it seems probable that limited impact was also felt at Levels II, III, and IV. It is difficult to avoid some, if small, changes at lower levels when a major change occurs at the highest level. In these terms, by 1954—two years after the termination of the Occupation—it appears that this trend had weakened considerably, and by 1959 it had been reversed and had returned to a "normal" pattern. Also, during the same period, the total proportion of higher officials having nonbureaucratic experience (see the total column) declined substantially, indicating a return to the tradition of low mobility in the Japanese bureaucracy.

INTER-MINISTERIAL TRANSFER

The concept of lifetime service encourages bureaucrats not only to remain in the government until retirement, but also to stay in the same ministry. Groups such as the "Foreign Ministry clique" or the "Home Ministry clique," mentioned in Chapter 4, could scarcely have existed without such a tendency. However, frequent and sometimes radical changes in government structure, especially during and after World War II, make it exceedingly difficult to measure inter-ministerial mobility, or even to define it clearly.

For our purposes, the significant kind of inter-ministerial movement is the transfer of individual officials occurring in a context not connected with a large-scale reorganization of the government or mass reassignment of personnel. Of these reorganizations and mass reassignments, there are two types of movement which technically constitute inter-ministerial transfers. The first type involves the transfer of sub-ministerial units, such as agencies, bureaus, divisions, and sections, from one ministry to another. The personnel of these units may move with them and continue to perform the same tasks, or they may remain in their original ministry and be reassigned to different tasks. Since the former involves crossing ministerial lines, it technically constitutes an inter-ministerial transfer even though no change of function occurs. The latter obviously does not constitute an inter-ministerial transfer, even though it does involve change of professional function.

The other type of movement occurs at the ministerial level when entire ministries appear and disappear, or are split or combined. In 1938, the old and powerful Home Ministry saw two of its many bureaus removed to become the nucleus of a new Welfare Ministry. In 1947 the Home Ministry was abolished altogether, and its functions were divided between the prefectural governments and other ministries of the national government, especially the Prime Minister's Office. Agriculture and Industry were long combined in a single ministry and then were split into two in 1925, were recombined in 1943, and were split again in 1945. The Economic Stabilization Board, a ministry in all but name, was created in 1946 and abolished in 1952, being succeeded by a smaller unit, the Economic Counseling Agency (*Keizai Shingi Chō*) with somewhat different tasks and objectives.[2] This ministerial type of reor-

[2] The Economic Counseling Agency in turn became the Economic Planning Agency (*Keizai Kikaku Chō*) in 1955.

98

ganization involves movements of personnel that technically constitute inter-ministerial transfers, although little or no change of function may be involved.

In any analysis of inter-ministerial mobility, the number of ministries in which a bureaucrat has served should be measured. It is, however, rather misleading to do so on the basis of the technical type of inter-ministerial transfers just described. When a ministerial reorganization or a mass reassignment takes place, officials may have no choice but to move to a different ministry in order to continue in government service. Such an approach would thus amount to an examination of government reorganizations plus a survey of what is generally regarded as inter-ministerial mobility of personnel rather than a measurement of the latter alone, and this problem is especially serious in view of the frequency of radical changes in the Japanese government. In order to discount such artificial movements of personnel, it is necessary to employ a narrower definition of inter-ministerial transfer. In this study, therefore, function is used as a limiting criterion in measuring inter-ministerial mobility. Whenever movements appear organizational in the above-indicated senses they are not counted as inter-ministerial movements unless accompanied by changes in function for the personnel concerned. Most inter-ministerial movements arising from reorganizations are therefore disregarded.

It should be stressed, however, that the major objective here is measurement of inter-ministerial mobility, not of functional mobility. Functional changes are normally ignored, therefore, unless a question of government reorganization appears to be affecting the issue of inter-ministerial mobility (there is high functional mobility within each ministry of the Japanese bureaucracy). An exception to the above rule is made in favor of service in sub-ministerial units which were once in the same ministry, but by the time of the survey had been assigned to separate ministries. For instance, past movements between the Construction Bureau and the Police Bureau in the Home Ministry are regarded as inter-ministerial movements so that they can be given as much weight as later movements between the Construction Ministry and the Police Agency of the Prime Minister's Office.

Table 29 shows the distribution of higher civil servants in terms of the number of ministries in which they had served up to the survey dates. A major feature in Table 29 is the stable pattern of inter-ministerial mobility. On the average (see the total row), approximately one-third of higher civil servants had served in only one ministry; another third had served in two ministries; and the remainder had served in three or more ministries. Of the last group, the largest subgroup, a quarter of the total, served in three ministries. In sum, the extent of inter-ministerial mobility appears to be considerably greater than is generally believed, and the proportion—slightly more than two out of every three higher administrators had experienced inter-ministerial transfer—seems to constitute a significant modification of the concept of lifetime service.

TABLE 29: DISTRIBUTION OF HIGHER CIVIL SERVANTS BY NUMBER OF MINISTRIES IN WHICH THEY SERVED, BY YEAR

	Number of Ministries					
Year	1	2	3	4	5 or more	Total
1949	35.8%	35.0%	19.1%	9.0%	1.1%	100.0%
1954	28.5%	31.8%	27.3%	8.4%	4.0%	100.0%
1959	29.7%	31.5%	26.9%	9.0%	2.9%	100.0%
Total	31.4%	32.9%	24.3%	8.8%	2.6%	100.0%

(N = 805; Levels I, II, and III; Core only)

However, Table 29 shows some chronological changes. The 1954 and 1959 distributions are similar, but the 1949 distribution is quite different. In 1949, relatively larger proportions of higher civil servants had been assigned to one or two ministries, while an appreciably smaller proportion had been in three ministries. Such

100

differences were apparently caused by the impact of the Allied Occupation and will be elaborated in the discussion of Table 30 below.

Two plausible but mutually exclusive hypotheses may be advanced concerning the relationship between inter-ministerial transfer and position level. Given the Japanese tradition of low mobility of labor, one may conjecture that frequent inter-ministerial movements would injure chances for promotion, and in many cases might involve a loss of seniority if not a drop in position level. On the other hand, one may speculate that the higher the position level of a bureaucrat, the longer his service, and the more likelihood of his having served in several ministries. When vacancies in the upper level in a ministry are few or slow in appearing, transfer to other ministries may offer the only practical alternative to rapid advancement. Since the extent of inter-ministerial mobility is somewhat greater than the concept of lifetime service implies, the latter hypothesis appears more promising. Table 30 deals with this problem.

TABLE 30: Proportion of Higher Civil Servants Who Had Served in Only One Ministry, by Year and Level

Year	Level				Total
	I	II	III	IV	
1949	41.3%	28.9%	40.2%	34.0%	34.4%
1954	28.2%	22.9%	35.9%	44.8%	41.2%
1959	23.1%	26.6%	38.4%	36.9%	35.0%
Total	31.5%	26.2%	38.3%	38.6%	36.8%

(N = 1,085; Core only)

Although the implications of Table 30 seem somewhat ambivalent, the figures may best be understood by a chronological review. The distribution for 1949 is appreciably different from those for 1954 and 1959, while the latter two resemble each other. The difference is especially large between 1949 and 1954 Level I. Also, for Levels I and II, rank-order is reversed between 1954 and 1959. The very high proportion for 1949 Level I apparently led to the moderately high proportion for 1954 Level I. By 1959, however, the proportion for Level II became greater than that for Level I. Thus, by 1959 or even to some degree by 1954, the proportion shows a negative, though weak, association with position level, while in 1949 the relationship is quite disturbed.

This indicates the existence of unusual conditions in 1949. As mentioned earlier, the 1949 distribution, especially its Level I figure seems to have been influenced by the American effort to recruit "outsiders" for higher positions in the bureaucracy. Although our data do not eliminate all the ambiguities with respect to this question, it is difficult to deny the impact of the Occupation on inter-ministerial mobility or many other features. On the other hand, the same data suggest that under "normal" conditions the extent of serving in only one ministry is negatively related to position level. In other words, the higher the position level of a bureaucrat, the greater the chance of his having served in other ministries, although it should be noted that the degree of association is fairly weak.

It may be expected that the degree of inter-ministerial mobility will vary more among ministries than among position levels. Table 31 sets forth data on this question. Although a complex set of factors are at work in Japanese personnel administration, it is clear that some of them are related to conditions peculiar to each of the ministries. Thus the movements of personnel among ministries are apparently affected by ministerial variations in recruitment policy, function, organization, and history. The relative prestige of a ministry also seems to influence such movements.

One major factor is the recruitment system. Most personnel surveyed in this study came to the civil service before the 1947

102

TABLE 31: PROPORTION OF HIGHER CIVIL SERVANTS WHO HAD SERVED IN ONLY ONE MINISTRY, BY MINISTRY

Core	Proportion	Proportion	Periphery
Justice	68.3%		
Telecommunications	66.7%		
Postal Services	55.6%		
		42.9%	Board of Audit
Agriculture and Forestry	42.2%		
Transportation	42.0%		
Foreign Affairs	40.7%		
Education	39.1%		
		31.7%	Ambassadors and Ministers*
		29.6%	Imperial Household Agency
Construction	28.6%		
Finance	23.5%		
Welfare	22.4%		
		21.2%	National Personnel Authority
International Trade and Industry	20.6%		
Economic Stabilization Board	13.8%		
Prime Minister's Office	13.6%		
Labor	9.5%		
Total (Core only)	31.4%		

(N = 997; Levels I, II, III, and diplomats)
* The figure for diplomats counts service in the Foreign Affairs Ministry and service in the diplomatic corps as service in only one ministry.

changes in the civil service regulations. The prewar higher civil service examinations were divided into three principal categories: (1) the judicial section, (2) the diplomatic section, and (3) the administrative section. This paralleled the division of the higher civil service into three principal career fields: (1) the Justice Ministry and the judiciary, (2) the Foreign Affairs Ministry and the diplomatic corps, and (3) all other ministries.[3] Transfer from one career field to another was possible, but it was more difficult than movement within the same field, and was limited to special circumstances. Although not all those surveyed in this study took the prewar higher civil service examinations, for most cases these three fields set gross boundaries for their career courses. Such career differentiation is clearly reflected in Justice's very high proportion serving in only one ministry. The proportion for Foreign Affairs is also relatively high; however, it is considerably reduced by the practice of assigning Foreign Affairs personnel temporarily to other ministries, especially Finance and International Trade and Industry.

A second major factor is functional specialization. A majority (68.5 percent) of higher administrators in Level III and above entered the service as "generalists" sharing a common training in law. Once in the bureaucracy, however, their diverse experiences took them in different directions and their initial assignments inevitably affected their potential range of inter-ministerial mobility. Those in such ministries as Telecommunications and Postal Services, or to a lesser degree Agriculture and Forestry or Transportation, acquired experiences and mastered tasks which were rarely relevant in the work of other ministries. Consequently the inter-ministerial mobility for men in these ministries remained low. Similarly, those recruited to the economic ministries—Finance, International Trade and Industry, and the Economic Stabilization Board—were functionally bound to economic matters. However, the fact that a good deal of functional similarity existed among the three economic ministries themselves contributed to a major scale

[3] In theory, officials of the Justice and Foreign Affairs Ministries (as distinguished from those in the judiciary and the diplomatic corps) were to be recruited through the administrative examinations. In practice, however, most were recruited through the judicial and diplomatic examinations, and entered the ministries only after serving mostly in the procuratorial or the consular corps.

of movement of personnel among these ministries. Moreover, men in these economic ministries occasionally went to non-economic ministries to handle financial and economic affairs, thus further increasing their inter-ministerial mobility.

A closely related factor is the functional scope of the ministry. The wider the scope of function of a ministry, the greater the possibility of inter-ministerial transfer. The Prime Minister's Office included a host of heterogeneous organizations, many of which were functionally related to one ministry or another. It is, therefore, to be expected that many men in the Prime Minister's Office would have served in other ministries.

A third major factor is the history or development of the Japanese bureaucracy. When a group of ministries shared a common origin, movements of personnel within that group tended to be frequent, even if they were functionally dissimilar. The high rates of inter-ministerial mobility for Labor, Welfare, and Construction were largely affected by this historical factor. In 1938 the Sanitation Bureau (*Eisei Kyoku*) and the Social Bureau (*Shakai Kyoku*) were transferred to the newly created Welfare Ministry. The Social Bureau was expanded, and a Labor Bureau (*Rōdō Kyoku*) was established in the Welfare Ministry. Although its title had been changed several times, this bureau became the essential basis of the Labor Ministry, organized in 1947. Likewise, the Construction Bureau (*Doboku Kyoku*) of the Home Ministry was the nucleus of the Construction Ministry, created in 1948. In addition, the Home Ministry supervised the police and local governments, and these tasks were transferred to the Prime Minister's Office in 1947, when the Home Ministry was abolished.

Because of the composite structure of the original Home Ministry and relatively high intra-ministerial mobility in the Japanese bureaucracy, men in the Home Ministry tended to acquire experience in many different functions through internal transfer and promotion. The trend continued to some extent even after new ministries were created out of the Home Ministry. Functional specialization was often ignored and transfer took place as if the original Home Ministry had still existed. The rates of inter-ministerial mobility for the Labor, Welfare, and Construction Ministries were thus largely raised by this factor. The proportion remaining in the Labor Ministry is, however, the lowest in Table 31. Since the two other ministries included more specialized personnel than Labor, and they moved less frequently than other officials, the figure for Labor was drastically reduced. The prewar and to some extent the postwar bureaucracy had very few labor specialists, but Welfare and Construction used medical doctors and engineers respectively.

In the periphery, the Board of Audit shows a low rate of inter-ministerial mobility. This parallels the Board's low ranking in the distribution of nonbureaucratic careers (Table 27). Also the figure for diplomats is appreciably lower than that for Foreign Affairs. The difference was caused by the fact that officials in the Foreign Affairs Ministry often transferred to other ministries before becoming ambassadors and ministers. The relatively low proportions for the Imperial Household Agency and the National Personnel Authority reflect the practice of recruiting men from a variety of fields including various ministries in the bureaucracy.

Inter-ministerial movements of personnel, however, must be examined further in terms of an apparent practice of transferring officials temporarily to another ministry mostly for training or acquiring special experience. In order to analyze the extent of this practice, Tables 32 and 33 measure concurrence of the first and the last ministerial assignments of higher civil servants, regardless of interim assignments. The "last" assignment means here the post which an official held immediately before retirement or in 1963, whichever came earlier.

A comparison of Table 30 (service in only one ministry) with Table 32 leaves little doubt as to the existence of a practice of

TABLE 32: PROPORTION OF HIGHER CIVIL SERVANTS WHOSE FIRST AND
LAST ASSIGNMENTS WERE IN THE SAME MINISTRIES, BY YEAR AND LEVEL

Year	Level				Total
	I	II	III	IV	
1949	69.6%	72.8%	67.5%	78.0%	76.1%
1954	64.1%	72.9%	70.7%	69.8%	70.0%
1959	64.1%	69.0%	70.9%	64.3%	65.5%
Total	66.1%	71.3%	69.5%	71.1%	70.8%

(N = 1,086; Core only)

transfer-and-return in the Japanese bureaucracy. While Table 30
shows that approximately one-third of postwar higher civil servants
remained in the same ministries throughout their careers, Table 32
shows that seven-tenths ended their service in the ministry where
they began. In other words, although about two-thirds moved
from the ministries in which they began their careers, more than
half of these eventually returned to their original ministries. Only
29.2 percent of higher civil servants were in different ministries at
the beginning and end of their careers.

It should be noted that position level and concurrence of first
and last ministerial assignments show almost no association; that
is, they are statistically independent. While Table 30 shows that
the frequency of permanent and temporary inter-ministerial transfers tends to increase as position level rises, Table 32 shows that
the extent of permanent inter-ministerial transfer is unrelated to
position level. In short, Table 32 shows that regardless of the position level a bureaucrat held in a given year, he had by and large
the same possibility of ending his career in the original ministry
as a man in some other level. Although probably not all of these
transfers-and-returns were concerned with any one purpose, the
practice of inter-ministerial transfer for apprenticeship seemed a
major pattern of these transfers.

However, there is reason to believe that this practice took very different forms in different ministries. Table 33 lists proportions by ministry of the higher civil servants whose first and last assignments were in the same ministries. Figure 5 compares temporary inter-ministerial transfer with permanent inter-ministerial transfer and nontransfer by combining data from Tables 31 and 33.

TABLE 33: Proportion of Higher Civil Servants Whose First and Last Assignments Were in the Same Ministries, by Ministry

Core	Proportion	Proportion	Periphery
Postal Services	100.0%		
Foreign Affairs	100.0%		
Telecommunications	95.2%		
Agriculture and Forestry	94.0%		
		93.3%	Ambassadors and Ministers*
Justice	92.1%		
Finance	90.1%		
International Trade and Industry	82.5%		
Economic Stabilization Board	75.9%		
		64.3%	Board of Audit
Education	56.5%		
Construction	53.6%		
Transportation	52.2%		
Prime Minister's Office	46.4%		
		29.6%	Imperial Household Agency
Welfare	28.6%		
		25.0%	National Personnel Authority
Labor	9.5%		
Total (Core only)	69.8%		

(N = 997; Levels I, II, III, and diplomats)

* The figure for diplomats counts service in the Foreign Affairs Ministry and service in the diplomatic corps as service in the same ministry.

5 · CAREER PATTERNS

FIGURE 5: INTER-MINISTERIAL MOBILITY OF HIGHER CIVIL SERVANTS, BY MINISTRY

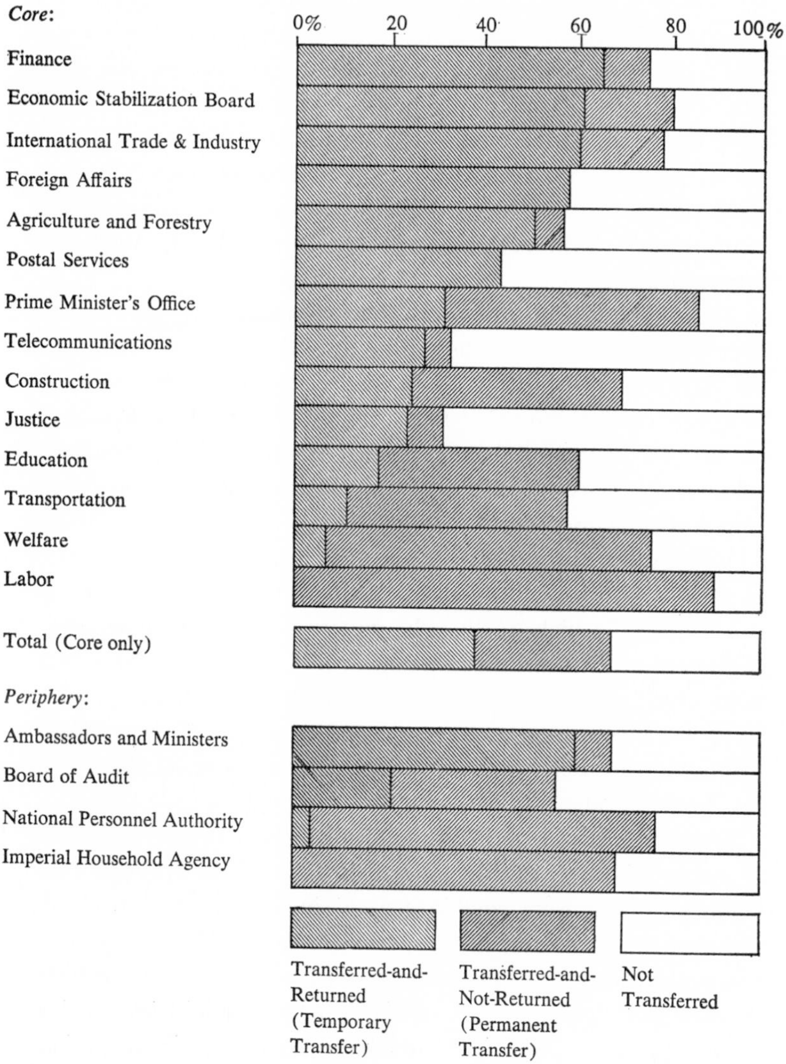

Transferred-and-Returned (Temporary Transfer)

Transferred-and-Not-Returned (Permanent Transfer)

Not Transferred

109

It is clear that the proportion of temporary inter-ministerial transfer varies greatly, the highest being 66.6 percent and the lowest being 0.0 percent. The three economic ministries together—Finance, the Economic Stabilization Board, and International Trade and Industry—stand highest in the list, suggesting that the practice of transfer-and-return was most commonly used in these ministries. Those in the economic ministries tended to be functionally useful in many other ministries, and were often transferred, but most returned eventually to their ministries. Also, the relatively high prestige of the economic ministries facilitated the high rates of returns.

The high rates of temporary inter-ministerial transfer for the economic ministries are followed by those for Foreign Affairs and for Agriculture and Forestry. In both cases, a majority of transfers were to the economic ministries or to the Prime Minister's Office. All Foreign Affairs personnel transferred temporarily to other ministries eventually returned. The purpose of apprenticeship was perhaps most effectively achieved in the Foreign Affairs Ministry, especially in view of the functional dissimilarities involved in transfer. In Agriculture and Forestry, inter-ministerial mobility is unexpectedly high, so that the pattern may represent an effort to give men of this ministry experience in a variety of outside positions which are concerned with agricultural matters. On the other hand, the low rate of permanent transfer for men in this ministry was affected chiefly by their relative functional specialization in the Japanese bureaucratic context.

For Postal Services, Telecommunications, and Justice, the degree of inter-ministerial mobility was very low. Postal Services and Telecommunications were combined as a single ministry until 1949, and their personnel rarely transferred elsewhere, except in recent years to such bodies as the National Police Agency or the Defense Agency as communications officials. In both ministries the low rates of permanent transfer were largely due to functional specialization of men in these ministries. Similarly, mobility for Justice Ministry officials consisted chiefly of movement to and from the procuratorial corps, which before the war belonged to a career field separate from the general administrative service. Even today most higher civil service posts in the Justice Ministry are by custom reserved for qualified lawyers. Permanent movement of personnel out of this ministry was thus limited. Most men, if transferred, went to the Legislation Bureau of the cabinet.

The three offspring of the former Home Ministry—Construction, Welfare, and Labor—stand very high in inter-ministerial mobility. As explained in connection with Table 31, the high rates were primarily due to their common organizational history. As far as the degree of temporary transfer is concerned, however, these ministries stand very low, indicating a less frequent use of the practice of transfer for apprenticeship. Since the original Home Ministry itself was abolished, men in those ministries less often returned to units which were parts of the Home Ministry. By and large, the relative rankings of prestige for these three ministries are low, and such a factor appears to be related also to the very high rates of leaving the original ministries permanently.

In the periphery, the pattern of inter-ministerial mobility for diplomats resembles that of higher officials in the Foreign Affairs Ministry. In both cases, about two-thirds of personnel transferred, but all or most of them returned. A small difference between the two is largely due to the fact that a few diplomats went to the Imperial Household Agency. While the Board of Audit shows a pattern not so different from the average for the core, the National Personnel Authority and the Imperial Household Agency show markedly different distributions. The National Personnel Authority had no counterpart before World War II, and its proportion of transfer-and-return is understandably very low. In the old Imperial Household Agency, however, no personnel are shown to have experienced the practice of transfer for apprenticeship. Its

111

higher officials were recruited from a variety of sources, including the Education, Foreign Affairs, and Home Ministries, but no official in this agency was sent back to these organizations or sent to others on a temporary basis. The periphery as a whole shows as much variation in inter-ministerial mobility as the core as a whole, again illustrating the heterogeneous composition of the periphery.

It is, however, difficult to conclude on the basis of our data that all those who experienced transfers-and-returns were always sent for the purpose of apprenticeship. Yet certain features are apparent in this pattern of temporary transfer. For example, the routes of transfers-and-returns were generally well established in the bureaucracy and, as illustrated above, were more rigidly followed than chance alone would dictate. It is probable that these movements were well known to the officials concerned in advance. It is also conceivable that most of these transfers were concerned with reasonably broad purposes rather than concrete and specific purposes, since the latter would tend to disrupt the standardization of transfer-and-return paths. It is thus unlikely that most of the personnel transferred were sent to teach specific skills or knowledge to specific groups, because such objectives could usually be fulfilled without much repetition. While some were sent simply because certain positions were reserved for men in certain other ministries, in many cases, as memoirs tell us, they were apparently sent to acquire experience and knowledge (thus improving their chance of advancement).

Transfer Between Field and Core

It seems, therefore, that inter-ministerial mobility of personnel is more limited than at first seemed to be the case: about one-third of postwar higher civil servants had always been in the same ministry, and another third began and ended their careers in the same ministry though transferring out and back again at some time. However, it is important to realize that intra-ministerial mobility was very extensive in the Japanese bureaucracy. Officials remained in one position for only short periods of time and then moved to other positions, in most cases in the same ministry. Some were assigned to field offices, others to units having very different functions in the core. Consequently total mobility—inter-ministerial plus intra-ministerial—was very high in the Japanese government. To demonstrate this we must examine, first, movement between field offices and the core, and, second, the term of office in a given position.

Most Japanese ministries have large networks of field offices spread throughout the nation, and the range of possible mobility is considerable even if one remains in the same ministry. In practice, movements between the core and the field are quite frequent. Two somewhat simplified hypotheses may be advanced with respect to such movements. The first is that the proportion of men with field experience would rise with position level, since longer service (higher position) means that there has been more opportunity for field service. The other, which is contrary to the first, is that assignment to a field office may reduce prospects for promotion or even result in permanent "exile" from the capital. Table 34 examines these hypotheses by presenting the proportion of higher civil servants with previous service in various field offices of

TABLE 34: Proportion of Higher Civil Servants Who Had Served in Field Offices, by Year and Level

Year	Level				Total
	I	II	III	IV	
1949	56.5%	68.4%	71.2%	71.0%	70.2%
1954	82.1%	67.8%	79.3%	65.6%	67.6%
1959	82.1%	75.5%	80.2%	75.0%	75.8%
Total	72.6%	71.1%	76.4%	70.4%	71.1%

(N = 1,087; Core only)

113

the bureaucracy. Our definition of field experience includes assignments to field offices of their original ministry as well as any other ministries during the period prior to each survey year. In practice, however, most movements between the core and the field did not involve inter-ministerial movements.

The results of the tabulation support neither hypothesis. The proportion for 1949 Level I is low because of the purge and the efforts of the Occupation to bring new men into the highest levels of the bureaucracy. Otherwise, the proportion tends to be stable regardless of survey year or position level. More than seven-tenths of postwar higher civil servants had served in the field at one time or another, and the extent of field-core movement was virtually unrelated to their position levels. Even those in Level IV had been in the civil service for at least fifteen or twenty years so that they had ample opportunity for assignments to field positions. Indeed, memoirs and biographies suggest that it was common practice to transfer prospective higher civil servants to the field without jeopardizing their future career. The thesis is further supported by the fact that in both 1954 and 1959 the proportions for Level I are slightly higher than any other level.

It is also interesting to note that field-core mobility (Table 34) is appreciably higher than inter-ministerial mobility (Table 30), and that the former is less correlated with position level than the latter. Thus a higher administrator was more likely to have served in the field than to have served in different ministries (temporarily or permanently). This implies that crossing ministerial boundaries was considered more serious than crossing the field-core boundary, especially if the former did not take place along the transfer-and-return patterns. Also, field-core movements were less related to position level than were inter-ministerial movements. This indicates that field-core movements took place largely irrespective of position level and at earlier stages of services than inter-ministerial movements.

TERM OF OFFICE

Another indicator of personnel movement is the term of office for a given position. A Japanese higher civil servant has traditionally been expected to move from one position to another fairly rapidly, especially if he is considered a promising official.[4] Sometimes mobility is so high that a bureaucrat assumes many different posts in a very short period of time. Within a ten-year period, for instance, one official in the Finance Ministry served as chief of a division supervising a public corporation, then became Chief of the Customs Bureau, Chief of the Secretariat of the Ministry, Chief of the Financial Bureau, Chief of the Foreign Exchange Bureau, Chief of the Banking Bureau, and was finally appointed Administrative Vice-Minister of the Finance Ministry. Another in the Foreign Affairs Ministry had an almost equally varied experience within a decade. He was first stationed in Argentina as Director of the Japanese Government Overseas Office, then came home to be in charge of war reparations to Asian nations. After again being sent overseas as Minister to Indonesia, he returned to become Chief of the Emigration Bureau, and ended the ten years by becoming Ambassador to Denmark. Although these two cases are not necessarily typical, they illustrate rapid lateral and vertical mobility within ministries, often without regard for functional specialization.

Table 35 measures length of service in the specific positions surveyed in this study. Although all the higher civil servants surveyed held a variety of positions during their careers, usually including several Level IV and often two or more at a higher level, Table 35 refers only to the tenure in the position held in the survey year. While data on terms of office are available in the biographical sources for only about half the 1949-1959 higher civil servants,

[4] Imai Kazuo, "Kanryō—sono seitai to uchimaku," Usui Yoshimi, ed., *Gendai kyōyō zenshū* (Tokyo: Chikuma Shobō, 1960), Vol. 21, p. 97.

the information, as will be shown presently, is apparently free from major biases. The distributions of these data show features by and large consistent with those of the distributions of other data in this study.

TABLE 35: AVERAGE TERM OF OFFICE, IN YEARS, OF HIGHER CIVIL SERVANTS, BY YEAR AND LEVEL

Year	Level				Total
	I	II	III	IV	
1949	2.9	3.6	3.7	3.0	3.2
1954	3.3	4.4	5.2	3.9	4.0
1959	3.3	3.1	3.1	2.7	2.9
Total	3.2	3.6	4.3	3.2	3.3

(N = 520; Core only)

Table 35 shows the average term of office, in years, of higher civil servants by survey year and position level. The overall average, considering all years and levels together, is slightly less than three and a half years. Although we lack comparable figures for the bureaucracies of other nations, the finding indicates rather brief terms, considering the importance of the positions surveyed and the lack of legal limits on terms of office. The average term (see the total row) is much the same in Levels I, II, and IV. Level III, however, shows a substantially longer term because this level included a number of specialists who remained in the same positions longer than others. Table 35 also shows a chronological variation. The 1954 average term of office at every level is greater than or equal to those in 1949 and 1959. Although the reasons for this are not clear, two primary causes may be suggested. The first is an extended result of reactions to the Allied Occupation. The second is the increase in the average age of higher civil servants. In 1949, as previously discussed, the Occupation exerted substantial influ-

116

ence in the upper echelons of the bureaucracy, which seemed to have resulted in the rather short average terms shown in Table 35. Although direct impact (removal) was largely limited to Level I, indirect impact (promotion, transfer, etc.) apparently spread to other levels of the higher civil service. Upgrading of others was bound to lower their average age and average term of office. In reaction to this, the 1954 higher civil servants tended to hold the same positions longer than their predecessors. In 1959, however, the short average term appears to have resulted from a different factor, namely, the increase in the average age of postwar higher civil servants.

A slightly different indicator of the rapidity of the movements of higher civil servants is the proportion of those who held the same positions for a given period of time. Tables 36 and 37 present the proportion of higher civil servants whose terms of office did not exceed four years.

Table 36 shows that on the average more than three-fourths of postwar higher civil servants moved from one position to another in four years or less, again indicating rapid movement in and out of important civil service positions. Table 36 thus supports and reinforces the results of Table 35. The proportions changing positions in four years are on the average (see the total row) not so different for Levels I, II, and IV, but the proportion for Level III is markedly lower than the others. Unlike Table 35, Table 36 leaves little doubt as to the special characteristics of Level III. Chronologically (see the total column), the pattern in Table 35 emerges also in Table 36, though the low mobility of the 1954 group is less marked in the latter. On the other hand, the high mobility of the 1959 group is magnified in Table 36, especially in Level IV, which was apparently most affected by the increasing average age of higher civil servants. In general, however, the chronological changes in tenure (see the total column) were less marked in

Table 36 than in Table 35. While both tables are useful in their own ways, the distribution in Table 36 indicates that the chronological changes were not as great as Table 35 alone suggests.

TABLE 36: PROPORTION OF HIGHER CIVIL SERVANTS WHOSE TERMS OF OFFICE WERE FOUR YEARS OR LESS, BY YEAR AND LEVEL

Year	Level				Total
	I	II	III	IV	
1949	79.3%	75.9%	62.2%	75.0%	74.3%
1954	77.4%	64.4%	41.7%	73.9%	70.9%
1959	80.8%	79.7%	53.3%	91.2%	87.7%
Total	79.1%	74.0%	52.4%	81.5%	78.6%

(N = 520; Core only)

Though lateral and vertical personnel movements were rapid in the upper bureaucracy, it seems that the extent of mobility varied considerably from one ministry to another. Table 37 shows the proportion of the higher civil servants by ministry whose terms of office did not exceed four years. The range of the variation is quite large: in some ministries almost all changed their positions in four years, and in some only one-third or one-sixth did so. Lateral and vertical mobility is affected by a variety of factors, and it is difficult to elaborate on every phase of this ministerial variation. However, some major features can be examined.

At first glance, it appears puzzling that the two ministries—Foreign Affairs and Justice—which provide the best opportunities to move into high positions in collateral categories should be at opposite ends of the spectrum. High-ranking bureaucrats in the Foreign Affairs Ministry traditionally joined the diplomatic corps, while those in the Justice Ministry often became judges or, more often, public procurators. In both instances, movement out of these ministries proper usually carried with it higher ranks and salaries than movement out of other ministries into their respective field

TABLE 37: Proportion of Higher Civil Servants Whose Terms of Office Were Four Years or Less, by Ministry

Core	Proportion	Proportion	Periphery
Foreign Affairs	92.3%		
Economic Stabilization Board	92.3%		
		83.3%	Ambassadors and Ministers
Telecommunications	81.8%		
Education	81.3%		
Construction	80.0%		
Finance	77.1%		
International Trade and Industry	76.3%		
Agriculture and Forestry	73.7%		
Welfare	70.8%		
Labor	69.2%		
Transportation	67.5%		
Postal Services	62.5%		
Justice	54.8%		
Prime Minister's Office	54.1%		
		50.0%	Board of Audit
		36.4%	National Personnel Authority
		15.4%	Imperial Household Agency
Total (Core only)	72.5%		

(N = 617; Levels I, II, III, and diplomats)

offices. Yet in Table 37 Foreign Affairs had a very high, and Justice a relatively low, proportion of higher civil servants with terms of four years or less. The reasons for this apparent paradox appear to lie in dissimilar circumstances and career courses in the two ministries.

Mobility in the Foreign Affairs Ministry has been greatly facilitated by the enormous postwar expansion in the number of embassies and legations. Ambassadorial appointments have been clearly considered more desirable than appointments to higher positions within the ministry at home, and consequently the direction of movement in the top levels has tended to be from the ministry to the diplomatic corps. In the Justice Ministry, however, there has been no comparable movement out of its higher echelons. The high prestige and comfortable salary of even lower levels of judicial and procuratorial positions have often drawn men from lower positions in the ministry in Tokyo, who might otherwise be pressing their superiors to move up or out to make room for them within the ministry. Once they become judges or more often procurators, they have been generally content to remain in the field, while in most ministries the ideal course has been to return from the field to assume positions of higher rank in the core. The low rate of mobility in Justice has also been influenced by a tradition in the judicial service: long terms have been considered normal and desirable because of the special nature of the judiciary and related offices.

The high proportions serving four years or less in the Economic Stabilization Board and the Telecommunications Ministry were largely due to the short lives of these organizations themselves. They existed only from 1946 to 1952 and from 1949 to 1952 respectively; therefore, few could hold the same positions for a long period of time. In two other economic ministries, Finance, and International Trade and Industry, more than three-fourths of higher civil servants changed positions in four years or less. As in inter-ministerial mobility, the degree of intra-ministerial mobility for the economic ministries was also high. In the Prime Minister's Office, nearly half held their positions for more than four years, partly because the agencies which made up this office were only loosely connected and did not interchange personnel like bureaus of a ministry. Men in the Cabinet Legislation Bureau, the Autonomy Agency, the Pension Bureau, and the Statistics Bureau tended to hold the same positions for long periods of time.

120

In the periphery, the proportion for ambassadors and ministers is as high as that for the Foreign Affairs Ministry. Since most Japanese diplomats began their service in the Foreign Affairs Ministry, the course of their careers tended to resemble those of officials in the ministry proper. In other words, diplomats moved as rapidly as those in the ministry, and transfers were probably more frequent in the Japanese diplomatic corps than in those of most other nations. In the remaining three units of the periphery, the proportions are extremely low, indicating a very different nature of mobility in the periphery as compared with the core. The proportion is lowest in the Imperial Household Agency, apparently reflecting not only a difference in outlook but also a difference in function.

MOBILITY AND SPECIALIZATION

Thus far, we have dealt with the movement of higher civil servants and shown that their total mobility—inter-ministerial plus intra-ministerial—was quite high. Postwar higher civil servants (Level IV and above) held the same positions for less than three and a half years, and more than three-fourths left their positions in four years or less. This pattern of transfer often ignored functional specialization. A higher administrator might supervise customs collection after regulating a public corporation, although the functions of the two were not similar. A diplomat serving as Minister to Indonesia might next become Ambassador to Denmark, regardless of the differences in social, economic, and political conditions in these two nations.

Such movements inevitably lead to the charge that Japanese bureaucrats tend to be inexperienced and therefore inefficient.[5] It may be argued that one is unlikely to be sufficiently familiar with conditions in both Indonesia and Denmark to be able to serve equally effectively in both countries. Similarly, it may be argued

[5] *Ibid.*, p. 106.

that one may not be equally competent in both supervising a public corporation and administering the collection of customs. In short, critics assert that efficiency in the Japanese bureaucracy is substantially reduced by rapid transfer in disregard of functional differentiation.

Yet it should be noted that these practices may also have positive consequences. For instance, reasonably rapid promotion may raise morale and thereby increase efficiency. Rapid transfer may not have created as serious functional problems as is often charged, since bureaucratic tasks were sufficiently standardized across the government organization, and routes of inter-ministerial mobility came to be sufficiently regularized to limit this trend. Also, rapidly advancing "generalists" were usually assisted by "specialists" working on a part-time basis or holding lower ranking positions. On balance, however, functional specialization appears to have been given less attention in the Japanese bureaucracy than in others so that the type of mobility found in the postwar bureaucracy may be undermining its efficiency.

This criticism is perhaps more meaningful than the Occupation's indictment of Japanese bureaucrats as incompetent because most of them had been trained in law. Japanese legal education, as indicated above, was considered a generalist training, and no other faculty offered courses which seemed any more appropriate for training prospective higher civil servants. A more relevant criterion in judging the competence of a Japanese bureaucrat, therefore, would be the extent and quality of the experience and training acquired after entering the civil service. Because faculties of law tended to attract the brightest students in Japan, potential higher civil servants were apt to be the kind of persons capable of acquiring specific qualifications for their positions after entering the service. This capability was, however, somewhat reduced by the practice of rapid transfer.

It must be remembered, however, that inter-ministerial mobility among higher civil servants was relatively low. Only about one-third transferred permanently to other ministries, and another third transferred only temporarily. Low inter-ministerial mobility was important in the sense that it limited the extent of transfer that totally ignored functional differentiation, and thus increased the opportunity for a prospective higher civil servant to acquire semi-specialized experience in a given set of fields. The degree of inter-ministerial mobility varied greatly from one ministry to another, but in many important ministries, the proportions of men permanently transferred to other ministries were especially low (see Figure 5). In Finance, International Trade and Industry, the Economic Stabilization Board, Foreign Affairs, Agriculture and Forestry, Justice, Postal Services, and Telecommunications, more than three-fourths of higher civil servants began and ended their careers in the same ministry (see Table 33).

Since ministerial boundaries in most cases served as a gross division of functions, low inter-ministerial mobility was a general safeguard against the kind of transfer which entirely ignored functional differentiation. The extent of specialization made possible by low inter-ministerial mobility was clearly less than usually expected in a modern organization or advocated by the reformers in the Allied Occupation. However, it should be recognized that the existence of these ministerial barriers to transfer provided important opportunities for the acquisition of specialized experience, and many Japanese bureaucrats profited greatly in an in-service training sense from such a pattern of transfer. Although most of them were trained in law, many in the course of their service became semi-specialized in fiscal matters, agricultural problems, postal questions and many other areas by the time they attained important positions in the bureaucracy. It would be erroneous to charge that Japanese bureaucrats were unqualified merely because they had studied law in college.

Yet it is difficult to believe that function has been the sole criterion in inter-ministerial or intra-ministerial movements of personnel. Within a ministry, or within a certain range of sub-units, as illustrated, the movements of higher civil servants tended to disregard technical functional differentiation. Sometimes function appeared to be a major criterion in transfer; at other times function was entirely unrelated to the patterns of mobility. Among the three economic ministries, for instance, functional similarities were very high. But very few moved permanently from one of the three to another (see Figure 5). Similarly, the involvement of those in Agriculture and Forestry in economic matters or in labor and construction problems was not reflected in patterns of permanent inter-ministerial transfer.

Although a variety of factors were involved in inter-ministerial mobility of personnel, factionalism among the ministries also appears to be an element of considerable importance. In the section dealing with education, we mentioned *shōbatsu* or ministerial cliques as well as *gakubatsu* or school cliques. These help to explain why there were few permanent exchanges of personnel among the economic ministries. Factionalism also helps to explain the strong tendency to transfer officials out temporarily and bring them back to their original ministries, and more importantly the low inter-ministerial mobility despite the high degree of homogeneity in educational background. The semi-specialization of Japanese higher civil servants apparently owed a great deal to factionalism among the ministries.

Years Since Graduation

Autobiographies and memoirs indicate that higher civil servants customarily identify their colleagues not so much by rank, position, or age, as by the year of graduation from a university.[6] Furthermore, it is widely believed that the year of graduation is a key

[6] Age is perhaps an inconvenient scale in measuring seniority since it increases every year.

criterion in promotion.[7] Seniority, in other words, is apparently less a question of age than of the time since graduation (or passing the civil service examinations). Table 38 presents data on this point. For analytical purposes, the number of years since graduation is used instead of the calendar year of graduation; the latter can be easily obtained by subtracting the average years in Table 38 from each survey year.

Table 38 shows a considerable correlation between position level and the number of years since graduation. As might be expected, the differences are smallest between Levels II and III, which are closest in ranking and salary. Also, Table 38 indicates that the average number of years since graduation has been steadily increasing in each of the four levels. For every five-year period, the average number of years since graduation required to attain a given level increased on the average by approximately two years (see the total column). As in the case of the average age of postwar higher civil servants, this is one of the most conspicuous chronological changes found in this study.

TABLE 38: AVERAGE NUMBER OF YEARS SINCE UNIVERSITY GRADUATION, BY YEAR AND LEVEL

Year	Level				Total
	I	II	III	IV	
1949	24.3	20.2	19.6	15.9	17.0
1954	25.6	22.1	21.2	18.3	19.2
1959	27.7	24.2	24.0	20.2	21.4
Total	25.8	22.4	21.4	18.0	19.1

(N = 1,078; Core only)

Since the year of graduation from university is a widely used reference scale, it is conceivable that years since graduation are

[7] Matsumoto Seichō, *Gendai kanryō ron* (Tokyo: Bungei Shunjūsha, 1963), pp. 17, 174.

more strongly correlated with position level than years since birth (i.e., age). In general, however, one would expect only minor differences between these two relationships, because years since graduation are highly correlated with age. Successful higher civil servants are likely to be men who graduated from universities without delays such as would result from failing in the higher school or university entrance examinations. Figure 6 presents a comparison of Table 12 (average incumbent age) and Table 38 (average number of years since graduation).

An obvious feature of Figure 6 is that incumbent age and the

FIGURE 6: AVERAGE AGE AND AVERAGE NUMBER OF YEARS SINCE
GRADUATION FROM UNIVERSITY, BY YEAR AND LEVEL

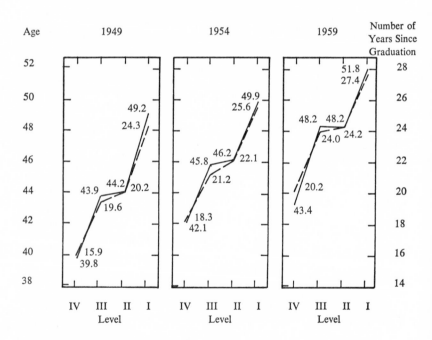

————— : Age
– – – – : Number of Years Since Graduation

126

number of years since graduation are very strongly correlated with each other, and the differences between the two are indeed minor. For many higher civil servants, the scaling by age and the scaling by years since graduation result in the same ranking. A careful examination, however, suggests that the correlation with position level is slightly stronger for years since graduation than for age. In every survey year, the line for years since graduation is somewhat closer to a straight line, which indicates a higher degree of correlation. Although other measures of association could be employed here, the above method will serve to indicate the general nature of the findings.[8]

The reasons underlying such distributions lie in recruitment and promotion patterns within the bureaucracy. There was no maximum age limit for taking the prewar higher civil service examinations or for appointment to the civil service. Yet nearly all who had successful civil service careers were men who had passed the examinations within a year before or after university graduation. Normally they entered the bureaucracy within a few months after graduation or passing the examinations, whichever came later. Those entering at the same time tended to advance at the same pace, regardless of age. The year of graduation was a customary form of identification and a factor of considerable importance in influencing promotion at higher levels of the Japanese bureaucracy.

PROMOTION

Promotion is, of course, a paramount concern in personnel administration, and here again the Japanese bureaucracy shows

[8] A standard method for this type of problem is Pearson's bivariate regression analysis. This method is, however, avoided here, since it is necessary to control other important variables before one examines the seniority system in the bureaucracy. Graduation from Tokyo Imperial University, for instance, is significantly related to promotion. Unless such variables are controlled, the importance of age or of the number of years since graduation in promotion cannot be precisely measured. See the section on promotion.

127

unique features. Promotion policy is critically related to the interests and performances of those staffing an organization, and an analysis of promotion policy provides valuable clues to the probable values and attitudes of Japanese officials.

There are several rather unusual aspects of promotion policy in the Japanese bureaucracy. First, it is virtually impossible to find a case in which a Japanese higher civil servant was demoted. Of 1,353 core and peripheral officials (Level IV and above) surveyed in this study, none is found to have moved to a position that was clearly inferior.[9] Second, the route and timing of promotion were often well known in advance. It was generally possible to anticipate when and to what post a bureaucrat would be promoted. A civil servant, for example, becomes a chief of section. At this level the General Affairs Section (*Sōmu Ka*), the Archives Section (*Bunsho Ka*), and the Accounting Section (*Kaikei Ka*) were considered superior to all other sections. An official who held one of these positions was marked for promotion to still higher levels. However, before attaining the bureau chief level, a bureaucrat often served as chief of a division or chief of secretariat. Some bureaus were more prestigious than others; in the Finance Ministry, for instance, the Budget Bureau (*Yosan Kyoku*) was considered more important than the Property Custodian Bureau (*Kanzai Kyoku*). The administrative vice-minister of a ministry was often selected from among the chiefs of important bureaus, while other bureau chiefs became chiefs of agencies. In every ministry, a pattern of this sort was visible and fairly stable in our data.

Although several variables were involved in the promotion of

[9] A few divisions are equal in importance to some bureaus, and are customarily headed by men of equivalent rank. Thus it is possible for a man to serve as chief of a major division after having been chief of a minor bureau. Technically he has moved from Level II to Level III, but actually he has kept or perhaps even improved his standing, both in rank and in influence.

higher civil servants, one clearly significant factor was university background. Figure 7 transforms Table 22 into a graph illustrating the importance in promotion of having attended Tokyo Imperial University.

Aside from the deviation for Level I in 1949 due to Occupation

FIGURE 7: Proportion of Higher Civil Servants Who Attended Tokyo Imperial University, by Year and Level

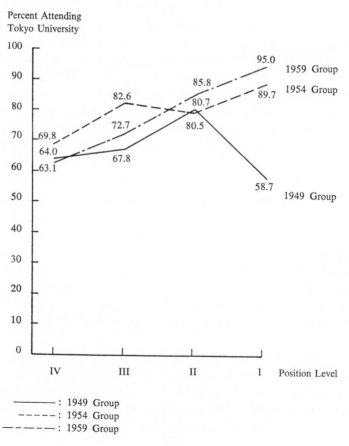

Percent Attending
Tokyo University

69.8 1959 Group
64.0 1954 Group
63.1

82.6

72.7

67.8

80.7

80.5

85.8

89.7

95.0

58.7 1949 Group

IV   III   II   I   Position Level

——————— : 1949 Group
– – – – – : 1954 Group
— – — – — : 1959 Group

129

policies, Figure 7 clearly indicates close association between position level and university background. The pattern is particularly remarkable for the 1959 survey group. The proportion attending Tokyo Imperial University increases steadily as position level rises, and at Level I there is almost complete dominance by Tokyo University graduates. Of the three survey groups, the 1959 group was chronologically most detached from Occupation influence, and the pattern in the 1959 group may be considered the norm of promotion in the Japanese bureaucracy.

Two other major factors were also involved in promotion: field of academic specialization and age. In Japan, "generalists" (i.e., law graduates) have been generally considered more qualified than "specialists" (i.e., engineering or literature graduates and the like) for higher supervisory positions in the bureaucracy or in business. Thus a considerable association was found between field of specialization and position level (Table 25). This belief in the superiority of generalists has been shared in Japan by students; and faculties of law, especially the Faculty of Law at Tokyo University, have usually attracted many of the brightest students.

An equally significant factor in promotion was age, which was regarded as an important indicator, other factors being equal, of the social and political rankings of individuals. Higher civil servants were rarely if ever actually demoted and were generally transferred and promoted in a steady and fairly standardized manner. Such a practice of personnel administration was closely tied to a traditional respect for seniority. Figure 8 incorporates these two factors in an analysis of promotion among the 1959 higher civil servants.

By controlling the two major variables, university and field of academic specialization, the relationship between position level and average age becomes more specified. It is evident in Figure 8 that those who attended the Faculty of Law at Tokyo Imperial University were quite regularly promoted from one level to another. The

130

5 · CAREER PATTERNS

FIGURE 8: UNIVERSITY, FIELD OF SPECIALIZATION, AVERAGE AGE, AND
POSITION LEVEL OF HIGHER CIVIL SERVANTS (1959)

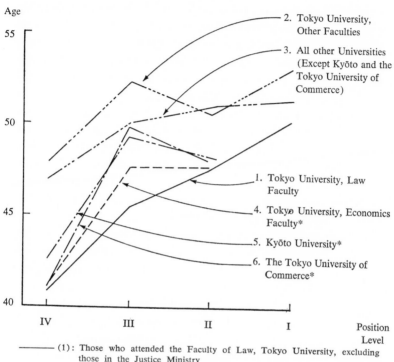

——————— (1): Those who attended the Faculty of Law, Tokyo University, excluding
those in the Justice Ministry
— - - - - — (2): Those who attended Tokyo University, excluding those attending its
Law and Economics Faculties
— - - - - — (3): All except those who attended Tokyo University, Kyōto University,
and the Tokyo University of Commerce
- - - - - - (4): Those who attended the Economics Faculty, Tokyo University
— - - - — (5): Those who attended Kyōto University
— - — (6): Those who attended the Tokyo University of Commerce
* Level I is omitted because of insufficient number of cases.

extent of association between their age and position level was far
stronger than for those with other educational backgrounds, while
they were at every level markedly younger than the others. In other
words, law graduates of Tokyo University were promoted most
rapidly and in closest conformance with seniority.

131

Figure 8 reveals other aspects of promotion as well. First, non-law (and noneconomics) graduates of Tokyo Imperial University tended to be older than graduates of other universities. It is rather surprising, in view of frequent criticisms of the *Tōdai batsu* (Tokyo University clique), to find that certain kinds of Tokyo University graduates were not promoted as rapidly as those of other universities. This is, however, not unusual because of the traditional belief in generalist superiority. It is this which accounts for the fact that nonlaw graduates of Tokyo University, who tended to be specialists in terms of education and function, advanced less rapidly than graduates of other universities, who tended to be generalists. The specialist tendency of nonlaw graduates of Tokyo University is also clear in an unusually high average age for Level III, whereas no comparable deviation is found for law graduates of Tokyo University or graduates of other universities.

Second, graduates of two well-known universities and a faculty, as shown in Figure 8, followed similar patterns of promotion, but all of them were noticeably different from the pattern for law graduates of Tokyo University. In published accounts, graduates of Kyōto University, the Tokyo University of Commerce, and the Faculty of Economics at Tokyo University are thought to be generally treated as important minorities against the overwhelming majority of Tokyo University Law Faculty graduates. There is an impression that these were the only exceptional groups "permitted" to reach the higher levels in the bureaucracy. Yet, as shown in Figure 8, they were promoted in a rather different manner. At every level, their average ages were higher than those of law graduates of Tokyo University, and they tended to be much older at Level III, suggesting that they held a different type of Level III position.

Among the 1959 group of higher civil servants, as classified by university or field of academic specialization, the group of law graduates of Tokyo University is most important in any further analysis of promotion. They undoubtedly constituted a dominant group among the 1959 higher civil servants (66.4 percent in Level III and above, and 50.1 percent in Level IV and above). They were the group most rapidly promoted, and their age advantage was as much as seven years, showing the critical significance of such educational background. Also, they were the group whose promotion most closely followed the seniority system. Thus, as will be explained presently, Pearson's correlation coefficient increases from 0.48 to 0.67, if the relationship between age and position level is measured only among law graduates of Tokyo University instead of for all 1959 higher civil servants.[10]

The last but not least important factor in promotion was a variable deriving from the organizational context. Throughout the preceding tables in this study, a considerable degree of variation was seen whenever data were tabulated by ministry. The average age (Table 13), for instance, varied remarkably and somewhat unsystematically from one ministry to another, but it varied in the expected manner if tabulated by position level (Table 12). More specifically, the pattern of promotion is likely to vary considerably from one ministerial setting to another, and the extent of conformity to seniority rules is likely to vary accordingly. By tabulating data by ministry, the ministerial variation is controlled, thus raising the correlation coefficient substantially. Figure 9 presents a graphic illustration of the computation of a Pearson's correlation coefficient between age and position level for the Ministry of Agriculture and Forestry, followed by Table 39 reporting a series of coefficients controlled by ministry.

The correlation coefficient between age and position level increases materially as each additional variable is controlled. The seniority system was followed more strictly among those who at-

[10] The range of Pearson's correlation coefficient is $-1.0 \leqq r \leqq 1.0$. For our purposes, however, it may be considered $0.0 \leqq r \leqq 1.0$, where 0.0 shows no association (independence) and 1.0 shows perfect association.

FIGURE 9: COMPUTATION OF CORRELATION COEFFICIENT FOR HIGHER
CIVIL SERVANTS IN THE MINISTRY OF AGRICULTURE AND
FORESTRY WHO HAD ATTENDED THE FACULTY OF LAW,
TOKYO UNIVERSITY (1959)

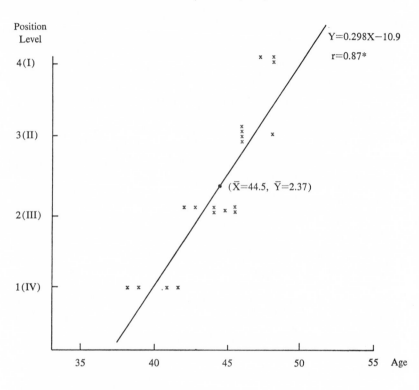

$$ ^*r = \frac{N\Sigma XiYi - (\Sigma Xi)(\Sigma Yi)}{\sqrt{[N\Sigma Xi^2 - (\Sigma Xi)^2][N\Sigma Yi^2 - (\Sigma Yi)^2]}} $$

tended the Faculty of Law at Tokyo Imperial University than
among the 1959 higher civil servants as a whole. The figure increases from 0.48 to 0.67, and the latter may be regarded as an
indication of rather significant association. The figure further increases to 0.75 if controlled by ministry, where such a high

TABLE 39: CORRELATION COEFFICIENT BETWEEN AGE AND POSITION LEVEL OF HIGHER CIVIL SERVANTS (1959)

All Higher Civil Servants	.48
Controlled by:	
Tokyo Imperial University, Faculty of Law	.67
Further Controlled by:	
Prime Minister's Office	.51
Justice	.73
Foreign Affairs	.92
Finance	.75
Education	—*
Welfare	.77
Agriculture and Forestry	.87
International Trade and Industry	.76
Transportation	.79
Postal Services	.80
Labor	.85
Construction	.95
Total (Core only)	.75**

* Insufficient number of cases.
** The average (mean) is computed as follows:

$$\bar{r} = \sqrt{\frac{1}{\Sigma n_i} (n_1 r_1^2 + n_2 r_2^2 + n_3 r_3^2 + \cdots + n_m r_m^2)}$$

coefficient suggests that in almost every ministry the seniority system was quite rigidly followed among law graduates of Tokyo University. An exception was the Prime Minister's Office, whose figure of 0.51 was markedly lower than the coefficient for any other ministry. The Prime Minister's Office, a collection of heterogeneous units, was something like a miniature of the whole bureaucracy itself. Its coefficient between age and position level could not be expected to be as high as those of other ministries.

As important a factor in promotion as age is the number of years since graduation. Indeed, most memoirs and studies of the bureaucracy do not mention age, but constantly cite the calendar year of graduation as a reference scale, and regard the number of years since graduation as a critical factor in promotion.[11] Such a term as "authority-balancing personnel policy" (*kenkō jinji*) refers to a pattern of personnel movements strictly in accordance with years since graduation, and suggests that years since graduation are more important than age as a factor in promotion.[12] On the other hand, age and years since graduation are heavily correlated, and one does not expect large differences between the two with respect to promotion. Most of those who eventually became higher civil servants completed higher school or university educations and passed the higher civil service examinations in about the same time so that age and the number of years since graduation are likely to show similar patterns of distribution.

Table 40 presents a series of correlation coefficients which are computed on the basis of the number of years since university graduation, instead of age as shown in Table 39. As might be expected, the average coefficient increases slightly from 0.75 for age to 0.77 for years since graduation. The specific values of the coefficients in Table 40 are very high except for two ministries. Again, the Prime Minister's Office, because of its heterogeneous composition, shows a markedly low figure. Personnel movements in the Justice Ministry were strongly influenced by those in the judiciary, and years since graduation were not as important in promotion as in other ministries. If we set these cases aside, the average coefficient for age becomes 0.77, and that for the number of years since graduation 0.86.

The differences between age and years since graduation as factors in promotion were then not as great as some accounts imply. One reason is that in most cases age and years since graduation refer, in substance, to the same numerical values, and heavy overlappings of the two sets of data do not lead to a major difference

[11] Matsumoto, *op.cit.*, pp. 17, 174.
[12] Imai, *op.cit.*, p. 106.

TABLE 40: CORRELATION COEFFICIENT BETWEEN THE NUMBER OF YEARS
SINCE GRADUATION AND POSITION LEVEL FOR THOSE WHO HAD ATTENDED
THE FACULTY OF LAW, TOKYO IMPERIAL UNIVERSITY (1959)

Prime Minister's Office	.50
Justice	.58
Foreign Affairs	.98
Finance	.84
Education	—*
Welfare	.84
Agriculture and Forestry	.93
International Trade and Industry	.76
Transportation	.91
Postal Services	.78
Labor	.84
Construction	.94
Total (Core only)	.77

* Insufficient number of cases.

in the coefficients. Also there is a practical advantage to using the
year of graduation rather than age in determining seniority. Since
it is fixed regardless of time, while age increases with time, the
calendar year of graduation is more convenient in ranking individuals. In our data, the number of years since graduation was generally more strongly correlated with position level than was age,
and the former was generally at least as much correlated as the
latter.

In this analysis of promotion, we have traced such factors as
university attended, field of academic specialization, organizational
context, age, and years since graduation. As the high values of the
correlation coefficients suggest, much of the pattern of promotion can be explained by these factors. Other variables are more
elusive: individual ability, performance, personality, relations
with cabinet ministers, and political situations. Biographical and
other accounts of the Japanese bureaucracy often devote much
space to these, especially personality and political context, and

often provide colorful and useful information on the working of the Japanese bureaucracy. The fact that our coefficients do not attain the maximum order (1.0) also suggests that the latter variables may account for the residual variance. However, in spite of the great attention paid to them, the former factors, as our statistical analysis shows, are more basic. In the Japanese bureaucracy, educational background and seniority were involved in promotion to a degree difficult to match in other major national bureaucracies.

Strict adherence to seniority in promotion inevitably invites a host of criticisms. Negativism, formalism, conservatism, and authoritarianism are terms commonly used in Japan in characterizing the Japanese bureaucracy, especially its upper echelons.[13] Although it is difficult to determine the validity of such charges on the basis of our data, the seniority system as practiced in the Japanese bureaucracy does lend them some credibility.

It is difficult to believe, however, that personnel administration was literally and mechanically based solely upon seniority. This is especially true if we broaden the scope of our observations. The totality of the Japanese bureaucracy consisted of a multitude of sub-organizations, located in various parts of the hierarchy and engaged in many different tasks. Given so large a number of units, it is difficult to maintain a uniform personnel system based strictly upon seniority. Indeed, even within a limited area such as the executive nucleus of the central government, we found a good deal of variation from one ministry to another in this respect. Furthermore, it is arithmetically impossible to conceive that every bureaucrat with certain characteristics would advance at the same speed. The higher the position level, the smaller the number of available posts. Large numbers of men necessarily failed to win promotion to Level IV and above. Thus, although it is true

[13] *Ibid.*, p. 65.

138

that in this study we found high correlation coefficients among those who managed to remain in the "main" stream, it also must be noted that the seniority rules were not observed as rigidly as it may seem, since there were many who either did not reach or did not remain in this stream, even though they possessed the same characteristics.

CHAPTER 6

Retirement

RAPID movement of personnel and a promotion system based chiefly upon seniority inevitably produced a massive outflow of higher civil servants from the Japanese government. Junior bureaucrats usually could not be promoted until their seniors vacated higher positions, and this tended to create pressures for early retirement. At the same time, the willingness of senior bureaucrats to retire at an early age depended in large part on the availability of reasonable alternatives to government service.

Certain conditions peculiar to Japan also affected this continuous exodus of postwar higher civil servants. First, the relevant laws and regulations encouraged early retirement, particularly by providing additional compensation for those who did so. Second, a host of semigovernmental organizations were created in Japan, especially after World War II, and retirement from the civil service often meant simply a transfer to such auxiliary units of the government. Third, Japanese higher civil servants, unlike their counterparts in some other nations, enjoyed considerable social and political prestige. They normally had little difficulty in finding alternative positions outside the bureaucracy. All these factors contributed to remarkably high outward mobility of Japanese higher civil servants.

Also, retirement sheds additional light upon personnel administration in the Japanese higher civil service. Although retirement is very critical in the careers of higher administrators, the process in Japan has seldom been legally regulated. As it is left largely to individual initiative, the manner of retirement provides a useful avenue for studying values and attitudes prevailing among higher civil servants. High standardization in this respect suggests that certain values and attitudes have been widely held and rigidly practiced by Japanese higher civil servants.

It should be stressed, however, that for many higher civil servants retirement, instead of terminating their active careers, launched them upon new careers in business, politics, and other fields. Retirement was, therefore, seldom final in a career sense. Having acquired a set of skills and established considerable reputation, retiring Japanese higher civil servants usually assumed important positions elsewhere in Japanese society.

Turnover and Retirement

Several methods can be used to measure the rate of outflow of postwar higher civil servants. One way is to examine the extent of the reappearance of the same individual in two or all three of the chronological groups studied. Figure 10 shows the proportions of higher civil servants remaining in the core after every five-year interval. Our data leave little doubt that the exodus from the three supervisory levels was massive and continuous. Approximately three-fourths of the 1949 group left the core within five years; about three-fourths of the 1954 group left within five years; and nearly three-fourths of those in the 1949 group who remained in 1954 had left the core by 1959. The entire pattern suggests, therefore, that the rate of turnover was rapid and stable throughout the 1949-1959 period.

Outflow from the core did not, of course, necessarily mean retirement from the civil service altogether. Some went to field offices of core ministries; others went to the periphery. It is desirable, therefore, to measure the rate of "absolute" turnover, or retirement from the civil service. Table 41 deals with this rate on the basis of four-year intervals. However, it is by no means always easy to define retirement from the civil service, and a brief explanation of

141

FIGURE 10: PROPORTION OF HIGHER CIVIL SERVANTS REMAINING
IN THE CORE, BY YEAR

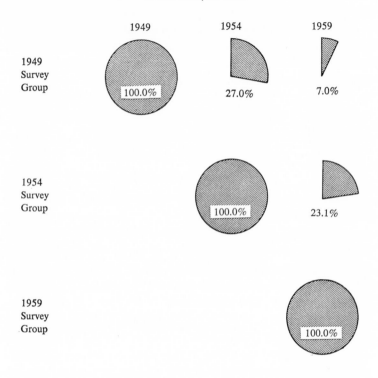

(N=820; Core only; Levels I, II, and III)

the definition used here is necessary. One major difficulty derives
from the broad scope of the National Public Service Law, which
classifies almost everyone paid from the national treasury as a
national public servant (see Figure 2). By this definition, one continues to be a civil servant even after becoming a cabinet minister,
a judge, or a professor at a national university. In this study, a
narrower definition is used; any movement out of the core or the

142

periphery, except to field offices of the core, is regarded as retirement. On the other hand, movement between the core and the periphery is not classified as retirement, except for movement from the Foreign Affairs Ministry proper to the diplomatic corps. Both the Foreign Affairs Ministry and the diplomatic corps are legally classified as separate services, and are somewhat different from each other in major characteristics.[1]

TABLE 41: PROPORTION OF HIGHER CIVIL SERVANTS WHO RETIRED
WITHIN FOUR YEARS, BY YEAR AND LEVEL*

	Level			
Year	I	II	III	Total
1949	71.9%	44.6%	30.1%	43.7%
1954	81.9%	45.9%	23.9%	43.7%
1959	89.0%	67.0%	48.9%	64.6%
Total	84.0%	56.8%	35.5%	53.6%

(N = 820; Core only)

* It is possible at this date to trace the 1959 group for only four years. Therefore, four rather than five-year steps are used for all survey groups. In five years, the total rates of retirement for the 1949 and 1954 groups were 52.5% and 54.3% respectively. Also note that the figures in the total row are close to the 1959 figures, for more data are available for the 1959 group.

The rate of retirement of higher civil servants, as Table 41 shows, is very high. Every year (see the total column), more than 10 percent left the bureaucracy, and on the average, more than half left within four or five years. The massive nature of this exodus is clearest at Level I, where from 70 percent to almost 90 percent left the service within every four-year period. The rate of retirement is, by definition, expected to be lower than the rate of turnover from the core, which was discussed earlier. By the use of these two rates, the outflow of postwar higher civil servants may be

[1] The Diplomatic Public Service Law, Article 2.

summarized. In every five-year interval, three out of every four higher civil servants left the core, and one out of every two retired from the civil service. Although comparable data for other bureaucracies are lacking, this pattern suggests remarkably high outward mobility in the upper echelons of the Japanese civil service.

Table 41 also shows a strong correlation between position level and retirement rate. As position level rises, the proportion retiring increases by a factor of from 10 percent to 40 percent. The increase is always positive, and its magnitude indicates a strong relationship between the position level of a bureaucrat and his chance of retiring. However, such a relationship is to be expected, since Japanese higher civil servants were promoted largely on a seniority basis. In order to maintain this type of promotion system and hierarchy of personnel, it is essential that a civil servant retire as he reaches a higher position. In addition, Table 41 suggests the possibility that the retirement age of postwar higher civil servants may be relatively uniform. Although the question cannot be answered by this tabulation alone, the fairly standardized pattern of retirement shown in Table 41 and the general importance of age in the bureaucracy imply that retirement age might be more uniform than, for instance, incumbent age.

RETIREMENT AGE

It should be noted that there has been no compulsory retirement age in the Japanese civil service.[2] The timing of retirement therefore sheds some light upon informal Japanese bureaucratic values and attitudes.

[2] Exceptions are judges and public procurators. The former are entirely omitted from the study; the latter are also excluded unless they concurrently held administrative positions in the Justice Ministry. The age limits for judges are from 65 to 70, depending upon level in the judiciary; those for procurators are from 63 to 65. See the Court Establishment Law, Article 50 and the Public Procurators Agency Establishment Law, Article 22.

Table 42 presents the average retirement age by ministry of higher civil servants. Since post-retirement opportunities varied considerably from ministry to ministry, the average retirement age also shows some deviation. The three economic ministries together stand at the bottom of the list, indicating that officials in these ministries retired from the service at the youngest ages. Those in Agriculture and Forestry also left the service quite early, as did those in Labor and in Transportation. On the other hand, the Education

TABLE 42: AVERAGE RETIREMENT AGE OF HIGHER CIVIL SERVANTS, BY MINISTRY

Core	Average Retirement Age	Average Retirement Age	Periphery
		67.5	Ambassadors and Ministers
		60.0	Imperial Household Agency
		57.9	Board of Audit
Justice	56.7		
		56.4	National Personnel Authority
Education	53.9		
Construction	52.0		
Prime Minister's Office	51.9		
Postal Services	51.6		
Welfare	51.4		
Foreign Affairs	51.0		
Telecommunications	50.8		
Transportation	50.7		
Agriculture and Forestry	50.6		
Labor	50.6		
International Trade and Industry	49.2		
Economic Stabilization Board	49.0		
Finance	48.8		
Total (Core only)	50.9		

(N = 650; Levels I, II, III, and diplomats)

Ministry has a high average retirement age while the Justice Ministry has the highest in the core. The ranks, salaries, and careers of those in Justice resembled those in the judiciary so that those in this ministry show the highest average age.

In the periphery, the average retirement ages are generally very high, and in most cases higher than any average in the core. The average for the National Personnel Authority is five years higher than the core average, while the figure for diplomats is sixteen years higher. It seems that the way senior bureaucrats in the periphery vacated positions for upcoming juniors was significantly different from that in the core. Such a difference in the process of retirement can be further examined in conjunction with the average incumbent age. Figure 11 combines Table 42 (average retirement age) and Table 13 (average incumbent age), as adjusted by the respective core averages.

In the periphery, the average retirement age spreads to a larger extent than the average incumbent age. More specifically, there was little tendency to standardize the time of retirement in the periphery, suggesting that little pressure seemed to have existed among seniors to leave the service at a given time and among juniors to be promoted regularly. However, Figure 11 conceals one aspect of the career pattern of diplomats that differed from other peripheral officials. Diplomats spent a good deal of time within the home country merely awaiting appointment orders. After becoming ambassadors or ministers, however, they moved to other positions at least as rapidly as core officials (Table 37), apparently because of pressures from below. In other words, diplomats were apparently expected to vacate their positions after a fairly short period of time; however, because of their irregular appointments they were not expected to retire at a certain age. Bearing this feature in mind, we see from the diagram that in the periphery the extent of variation in the average retirement age is clearly higher than in the average incumbent age.

146

FIGURE 11: DEVIATION OF AVERAGE INCUMBENT AGE AND AVERAGE
RETIREMENT AGE FROM RESPECTIVE CORE AVERAGES, BY MINISTRY*

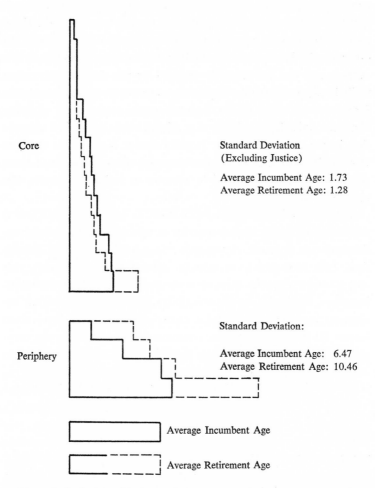

Core

Standard Deviation
(Excluding Justice)

Average Incumbent Age: 1.73
Average Retirement Age: 1.28

Periphery

Standard Deviation:

Average Incumbent Age: 6.47
Average Retirement Age: 10.46

Average Incumbent Age

Average Retirement Age

* For each distribution, ministries are ranked in terms of the extent of deviation from
the respective average. The interval therefore does not necessarily represent the same
ministry for both deviations.

147

In the core, however, the average retirement age tends to be more standardized, and shows less deviation from the average incumbent age, except in the Justice Ministry. The standard deviation for the former is 2.01, while that for the latter is 1.99. If we exclude Justice, the respective figures become 1.28 and 1.73. In other words, in the core (excluding Justice) the variation in the average age was considerably reduced by the time of retirement, while in the periphery the opposite was true. It is evident that some forces were at work in the Japanese upper bureaucracy to bring about a standardization in the time of retirement. Figure 11 suggests that in the core (excluding Justice) senior higher civil servants were under strong pressures to leave the service at a given time, while juniors were expected to advance as rapidly as senior officials had advanced.

Yet the trend toward standardization, as seen in Figure 11, was not complete, and a certain amount of variation in the average retirement age remains. To pursue this question, another tabulation, Table 43, shows the average retirement age by survey year and position level. In spite of some positional and chronological increases, Table 43 shows remarkable stability in the average retirement age. The positional increase (see the total row) from Levels III to I in the average retirement age is less than the comparable increase in the average incumbent age (see Table 12). In

TABLE 43: AVERAGE RETIREMENT AGE OF HIGHER CIVIL SERVANTS, BY YEAR AND LEVEL

	Level			
Year	I	II	III	Total
1949	51.7	49.3	50.1	50.1
1954	52.8	50.7	51.3	51.3
1959	53.6	51.0	51.4	51.5
Total	52.6	50.3	50.9	50.9

(N = 573; Core only)

148

Chapter 3, we reported the steady chronological increase in the average age of higher civil servants. However, the chronological increase in the average retirement age is less than half the increase in the average age. This suggests that traditional pressures for retirement at a certain age continued despite the increase in the average age of incumbents, and that the prevailing values and attitudes in the bureaucracy were highly resistant to such a potentially powerful force for change as the increase in incumbent age.

Although the pressures of the increasing average age brought about only limited effects on the average retirement age, its overall impact must not be underestimated, especially in view of the importance of seniority in the Japanese bureaucracy. In part, the chronological age increase apparently resulted in an increasing rate of retirement of higher civil servants. Table 41 shows nearly a 50 percent increase in rate of retirement from 1954 to 1959, and Figure 12 shows the constant nature of this increase. By and large, the rate of retirement for each survey group shows linearity, while the differences between the 1959 group and the 1949 or 1954 group are almost always as large as 50 percent. The importance of age was demonstrated in the section dealing with promotion. In retirement, it seems that the impact of the increasing average age was similarly profound, and apparently contributed to an exodus of higher civil servants at a rate one and a half times as fast as in the two preceding survey groups.

However, the differences in rate of retirement between the 1949 and 1954 groups are much less than those between the 1959 group and both the 1949 and 1954 groups. This apparent irregularity in the increase in rate of retirement may be examined in terms of incumbent age and retirement age. A small increase in rate of retirement from 1949 to 1954 is compensated for by great increases in the average age (see Table 12) as well as in the average retirement age (see Table 43) in the same period. Similarly, a great increase in rate of retirement from 1954 to 1959 is balanced by small in-

149

FIGURE 12: Stability and Change in Retirement Rate of
Higher Civil Servants, by Year

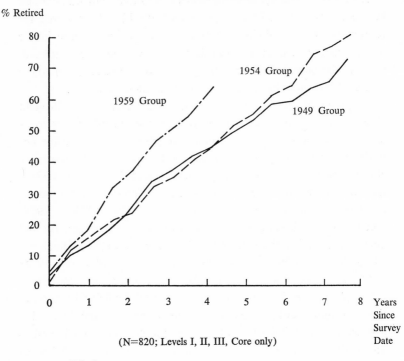

% Retired

(N=820; Levels I, II, III, Core only)

—————: 1949 Group
– – – – –: 1954 Group
— – — –: 1959 Group

creases in the average incumbent age and the average retirement age. Although incumbent age and retirement age do not account for all the variation in the movement of personnel, these factors certainly exert, as seen in the analysis of promotion, profound influence in the Japanese upper bureaucracy, and they apparently affect some of the major aspects of the outflow of higher civil servants.

150

Although postwar higher civil servants maintained reasonably similar average ages of retirement, their average incumbent age increased slowly but steadily during the same period. An unavoidable question is whether or not they will continue to maintain similar retirement ages by increasing the rate of retirement as radically as between 1954 and 1959. Although there was a powerful trend to maintain the status quo in the bureaucracy, the long-term effect is likely to be negative at least in the sense of a slow and gradual increase. A part of the answer is seen in the table of the average retirement age by year and level (Table 43). As shown in the total column, the average retirement age increased one and a half years in the 1949-1959 period. Steady increases are seen in every five-year interval and in every position level, though the greatest net gain is found in Level I.

Another part of the answer is found in Figure 13, which shows stability and change in the average retirement age longitudinally. On the whole, Figure 13 indicates high stability in the average retirement age. Postwar higher civil servants retired at similar ages regardless of how long they remained in the bureaucracy after 1949, 1954, or 1959. The powerful tendency to maintain similar average retirement ages is again demonstrated in this tabulation. Yet the same data give some indications of the gradual increase in the average retirement age. The 1954 average line moved somewhat upward from the 1949 line. The average for the 1959 group generally resembled that of the 1954 group until the third year after the survey date, but suddenly increased in the fourth year. The combined effect of these increases in the average incumbent age was then to bring about a slow but steady increase in the average retirement age, although this trend seemed to be strongly resisted by traditional values and attitudes in the bureaucracy.

It is difficult to dismiss the powerful nature of this resistance. Age (for incumbency or retirement) is apparently a deep-rooted factor in the Japanese higher civil service; it cannot be radically

151

FIGURE 13: STABILITY AND CHANGE IN AVERAGE RETIREMENT AGE
OF HIGHER CIVIL SERVANTS, BY YEAR

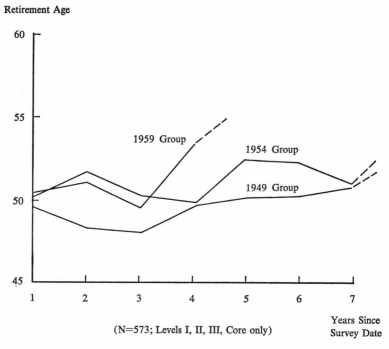

Retirement Age

(N=573; Levels I, II, III, Core only)

Years Since
Survey Date

changed without exerting profound impact upon the higher civil
service as a whole. The significance of these factors is illustrated
by the fact that age is closely related to the relative positions of
the ministries in the Japanese bureaucracy. Throughout this study
data were tabulated mostly by survey year, position level, and ministry. Of the three, the last yielded the greatest variation for nearly
every variable. This in turn suggests that the ministries are an
important underlying variable, although not readily susceptible to
quantification. Figure 14 presents one of the approaches in coping
with this question in terms of the average incumbent age and the
average retirement age.

152

FIGURE 14: RANKING OF ORGANIZATIONS IN CORE AND PERIPHERY,
BY AVERAGE INCUMBENT AGE AND AVERAGE RETIREMENT AGE

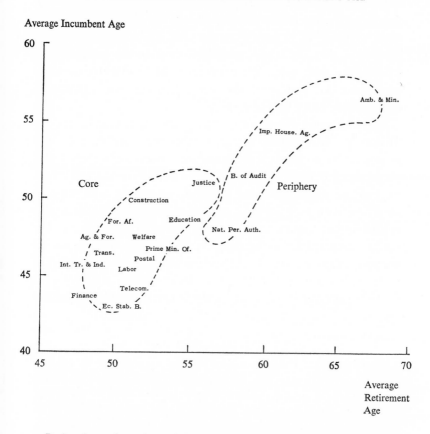

It is clear that the ministries placed in this two-dimensional scale closely approximate the expected ordering of the ministries. The core ministries are relatively clustered, while the peripheral units are widespread. This corroborates our general finding that core officials tend to be homogeneous, while peripheral officials tend to be heterogeneous. Also, Figure 14 shows that the core ministries tend to occupy one general area whereas the peripheral units oc-

153

cupy another. This ordering supports our initial research strategy in this study to separate the core from the periphery. An exception is the Justice Ministry, which should be, on the basis of this scale, classified as a peripheral unit. For the reasons mentioned previously, those in Justice resembled those in the judiciary and followed a career quite different from those in other core ministries. From this standpoint, the Justice Ministry should belong to the periphery rather than to the core.

The reasons for this fit where such a scale is concerned are not difficult to find. Japanese higher administrators are by and large homogeneous in terms of the universities where they studied and the academic fields in which they specialized. Hence age and ministry, the two major remaining variables, are bound to be strongly correlated with each other. Age (for incumbency or retirement) is thus related to ministerial cliques (*shōbatsu*), which is another major characteristic of the Japanese bureaucracy. Earlier we reported a steady increase of the average age of postwar higher civil servants, but it should be expected that a variable as deep-rooted in the organizational structure as age is not susceptible to radical change.

POST-BUREAUCRATIC OCCUPATION

Postwar higher civil servants retired, on the average, at age fifty or fifty-one. However, men of fifty had an average life expectancy of another 21.5 years in 1949 and 22.7 years in 1959.[3] An obvious reason for early retirement is that prospects for subsequent employment have traditionally been excellent. Very few of those who retired became entirely inactive; most entered other fields, and many obtained positions or salaries comparable to or higher than those in the civil service. Such bright prospects, in turn, have been related to the general social and political status of higher civil servants, and have also influenced university students in choosing the

[3] *Japan Statistical Yearbook*, 1961 ed., pp. 36-37.

civil service as a career. In the postwar period, however, the prestige of higher civil servants appears to have been somewhat reduced, and a decline in their post-bureaucratic prospects was partially offset by the expansion of opportunities for transferring to public corporations. Table 44 shows a distribution of post-bureaucratic occupations by survey year.

As shown in the total column of Table 44, approximately three-tenths of retiring higher civil servants went to public corporations and another three-tenths into business. The remainder, about four-tenths, entered eight different fields. A few became judges or Diet employees (but not Diet members), who are, for convenience, included in the category of government committees. Those entering a profession include those who became attorneys, notaries public, and practicing medical doctors. Most of those who entered local governments became prefectural governors. Among those whose post-retirement career could not be identified, a few apparently became entirely inactive after leaving the service, but a large propor-

TABLE 44: DISTRIBUTION OF HIGHER CIVIL SERVANTS BY POST-BUREAUCRATIC OCCUPATION, BY YEAR

Occupation	1949	1954	1959	Total
Public Corporations	25.7%	35.3%	30.3%	30.1%
Business	30.9%	27.2%	29.4%	29.2%
Ambassadors and Ministers	6.0%	6.3%	8.1%	6.7%
Government Committees and others	3.8%	8.6%	7.0%	6.3%
Diet Members	6.4%	6.3%	4.3%	5.8%
Nonprofit Organizations	5.3%	4.5%	5.4%	5.1%
Professions	4.5%	4.5%	5.2%	4.8%
Educators	4.2%	1.4%	2.2%	2.7%
Local Government	4.9%	0.5%	0.5%	2.2%
Agriculture	0.4%	0.0%	0.0%	0.1%
Unknown	7.9%	5.4%	7.6%	7.0%
Total (Core only)	100.0%	100.0%	100.0%	100.0%

(N = 671; Levels I, II, and III; Core only)

155

tion—perhaps as high as a half—appear to have died during the service or soon after retiring.

The distributions of post-bureaucratic occupations are on the whole similar from one survey group to another. Public corporations and business were the two principal fields that the 1949-1959 higher civil servants entered upon retirement. Although the relative ranking of the two in the 1949 group is reversed in the 1954 and 1959 groups, the difference is small. In Table 44 alone it is not clear whether there were some major changes in post-retirement prospects.

Tables 45 and 46 present distributions by ministry of higher civil servants entering business and public corporations. The proportions entering business from International Trade and Industry and the Economic Stabilization Board are, as might be expected, very high. The proportions for Transportation, Telecommunications, and Postal Services are also high, but the types of business tend to differ depending upon the function of the ministry from which they were retiring. Those retiring from Transportation went chiefly to private transportation corporations (railroad, bus, or shipping). Those from Telecommunications and Postal Services similarly found positions in private communication and sometimes in transportation companies. However, higher civil servants retiring from the economic ministries mostly entered heavy industry, major banking, or large trade corporations, most of which were formerly associated with the *zaibatsu* or financial combines. Post-retirement opportunities often had an obvious connection with pre-retirement duties in the civil service, and there were few regulations to control this.

A surprising feature in Tables 45 and 46 is that only a small proportion of those retiring from Finance went into business, while a very large proportion went to public corporations. Traditionally, the Finance Ministry has been regarded as one of the most prestigious ministries, and its higher officials have had bright pros-

TABLE 45: Proportion of Higher Civil Servants Who Entered
Business upon Retirement, by Ministry

Core	Proportion	Proportion	Periphery
International Trade and Industry	59.1%		
Transportation	42.9%		
Economic Stabilization Board	37.9%		
Telecommunications	37.5%		
Postal Services	36.8%		
Agriculture and Forestry	33.3%		
		28.6%	Ambassadors and Ministers
Prime Minister's Office	25.9%		
Construction	23.1%		
Finance	19.7%		
		14.3%	National Personnel Authority
Welfare	7.5%		
Justice	7.1%		
Education	5.6%		
		5.6%	Board of Audit
Foreign Affairs	0.0%		
Labor	0.0%		
		0.0%	Imperial Household Agency
Total (Core only)	29.2%		

(N = 752; Levels I, II, III, and diplomats)

pects after retirement. The small proportion entering business is
thus somewhat incongruous, and may indicate that increasing functional specialization in business is creating a demand for men with
more explicit experience in business affairs. It may also reflect the
general decline in the social and political prestige of higher civil
servants since the war.

In any event, about three-tenths, or the largest single group, of
all retiring higher civil servants went to public corporations dur-

TABLE 46: Proportion of Higher Civil Servants Who Entered
Public Corporations upon Retirement, by Ministry

Core	Proportion	Proportion	Periphery
Finance	66.7%		
Telecommunications	50.0%		
Labor	43.8%		
Postal Services	39.5%		
Construction	38.5%		
Transportation	38.1%		
Economic Stabilization Board	34.5%		
Prime Minister's Office	32.4%		
		28.6%	National Personnel Authority
Welfare	25.0%		
		23.5%	Board of Audit
International Trade and Industry	18.2%		
		16.7%	Imperial Household Agency
Agriculture and Forestry	16.0%		
Education	5.6%		
Foreign Affairs	0.0%		
Justice	0.0%		
		0.0%	Ambassadors and Ministers
Total (Core only)	30.1%		

(N = 752; Levels I, II, III, and diplomats)

ing the 1949-1959 period. This suggests general difficulties in secur-
ing lucrative private employment. Certain institutional changes
after the war also affected the careers of higher civil servants. Prefectural governorships, formerly appointive, became elective, and
election to the Diet became almost essential to appointment as a
cabinet minister. Thus it is now more difficult for a career bureaucrat to become a governor or cabinet minister than before the
war. All these conditions seem to have contributed to the high

158

rate for entering public corporations and the steady increase in the average age of higher civil servants.

Some ministries were scarcely related to either business or public corporations, and very few of their retiring officials went to these fields. The Justice and Education Ministries are examples of this. Most of those from Justice became practicing attorneys, and those from Education went to nonprofit organizations and educational institutions. Officials in the Imperial Household Agency were performing rather unique functions, and none went to business after retiring, though a few went to public corporations. All officials retiring from the Foreign Affairs Ministry became ambassadors or ministers, and this movement was facilitated by the expansion of Japanese overseas missions during the postwar period.

A common feature of the post-bureaucratic occupations of higher civil servants is high rank. Retiring officials who went into business generally became members of boards of directors, often in very large corporations. Others became presidents or vice-presidents of public corporations and nonprofit organizations. Some were appointed professors or presidents of institutions of higher learning. Some returned to their home prefectures and were elected governors or Diet members. Officials in Foreign Affairs became ambassadors and ministers; conversely, there were very few postwar Japanese diplomats who were not former career bureaucrats in this ministry. The general status of higher civil servants may be declining and their prospects may be somewhat restricted by institutional changes since the war, but there is little question as to the overall superior standing of Japanese higher civil servants. In few major nations have retired bureaucrats moved into so many important positions in so many areas. Consequently, postwar higher civil servants in Japan have played an important role in the economic, political, and social field even after retiring from the civil service.

CHAPTER 7

The Postwar Japanese Bureaucracy

THE present study has examined the social origins, educational backgrounds, and career patterns of the 1949-1959 Japanese higher civil servants. In Chapter 2 the rationale for selecting specific positions for study and analysis—and therefore specific individuals—was explained. In Chapters 3 through 6 the major characteristics of this sample of the higher bureaucracy were statistically examined and interpreted. We now turn to a review of the overall implications of our data and the position of the Japanese bureaucracy in a broader context.

SOCIAL ORIGINS

Historically, higher officials in Japan had been recruited from a narrow social base. However, our data indicate that the social origins of postwar higher civil servants were largely heterogeneous. They were more or less proportionately recruited from all parts of Japan, although more came from towns and cities than from villages. Tokyo, however, supplied a disproportionately large share. A few were related by birth or marriage to eminent families, but a large majority appear to have come from what might be called the middle class. Among those related to eminent families, the occupations of their fathers and fathers-in-law were remarkably diverse. A very small group had held positions of bureaucratic or political leadership. Although these eminent families supplied a larger proportion of higher civil servants than its proportion in the national population would lead one to expect, none of our data suggest that any one social or political group in Japan provided a

160

dominant share of higher administrators, or that any significant number of families supplied higher civil servants in several successive generations.

Such diversity is likely to be characteristic of the bureaucracy in any modern nation where traditional forms of social stratification have largely disappeared. The Meiji government eliminated most of the formal feudal distinctions and discriminatory barriers in the early years so that the Japanese people were at that time generally guaranteed equality before the law. Also, the Meiji government provided more meaningful paths of social mobility by establishing the modern educational system and the higher civil service examinations system. The cumulative results of these factors have been profound, and in general they account for the heterogeneous social origins of postwar higher civil servants.

This heterogeneity, however, must also be reviewed in a broader perspective. The Japanese people are remarkably homogeneous in ethnic origin, language, religion, and regionalism. The factor of heterogeneous social origins is thus not as important in Japan as in some other nations, and its significance should not be overestimated in evaluating the modern Japanese. It is largely counterbalanced by homogeneity in other factors, especially in education.

EDUCATIONAL BACKGROUNDS

While the social base for recruitment of the bureaucratic elite was expansive, the educational base was very narrow. As a result, diversities in their social origins were offset or more than offset by similarities in their education. Before discussing the quantitative aspects, it is important to summarize the qualitative aspects of educational homogeneity in Japan. First, education is generally regarded as a very important factor in forming values and attitudes in any nation. In Japan this trend has been reinforced by the lack of major diversities in ethnic origin, language, religion, and region-

161

alism. Second, the leveling influence of education was particularly great in Japan, since the prewar educational system was centrally controlled and hierarchically structured. Consequently education in Japan tended to result in greater homogeneity than in other nations. Finally, education has been traditionally respected, and is highly related to social status in modern Japan. University education, especially Tokyo Imperial University education, has been an important factor in producing a variety of elites in Japan.[1] Tokyo University graduates may thus be regarded as a subcultural group providing a large part of the top leadership in modern Japan.

Quantitatively, the extraordinary degree of educational homogeneity is scarcely a matter of debate. Approximately four-fifths (Level III and above) of postwar higher civil servants attended Tokyo Imperial University. Although the proportion varied according to the manner of tabulation, it was seldom less than 50 percent regardless of position level, survey year, and location in core or periphery. The extent of this dominance by graduates of a single university is staggering even in comparison with the combined share for Oxford and Cambridge in the British bureaucracy. In Japan, Tokyo University is often called the *kanryō yōseijo* or "nursery for bureaucrats."

Educational homogeneity is also high in terms of the field of specialization at the university level. About two-thirds (Level III and above) attended faculties of law, and more than half attended the Faculty of Law at Tokyo University. In Japan, generalists (i.e., law graduates) are usually preferred to specialists (i.e., engineering graduates, literature graduates, and the like) for senior supervisory positions in the bureaucracy or in business. The high proportion of law graduates among postwar higher administrators corroborates the widespread belief of the "omnipotence of legal studies" (*hōka bannō*). All in all, this remarkably high educational

[1] Asō, *op.cit.* (*Nihon Ikueikai Kenkyū Kiyō*), p. 71; Inoki, *op.cit.*, p. 296.

homogeneity constitutes one of the most important characteristics of postwar Japanese higher civil servants.

CAREER PATTERNS

One consequence of high educational homogeneity is the standardization of the career patterns of higher civil servants. This is most pronounced in the processes of promotion and retirement. Promotion in the higher civil service was largely accounted for by university attended, field of academic specialization, and number of years since graduation (or age). In other words, men were generally marked for advancement by educational background, and were generally promoted by seniority among the ranks of those with similar education. This pattern was particularly clear among the 1959 group of higher civil servants.

Similarly, the process of retirement was highly standardized. Postwar higher civil servants left the bureaucracy at similar ages, although the steady rise in the average age was apparently influencing the rate of retirement. Since men of fifty or fifty-one were expected to live another twenty years, retirement usually meant termination of their bureaucratic careers in the prime of life. Yet the rate of retirement was remarkably high, indicating not only massive outward mobility from the bureaucracy but also rapid mobility within the higher civil service itself. In view of the lack of meaningful legal or institutional standards, the whole process of outward and upward movement was apparently based upon bureaucratic values and attitudes. The extent of standardization suggested the rigidity with which these values and attitudes were held and practiced in the Japanese higher civil service.

Lateral (inter-ministerial) mobility is, however, less evident than vertical (intra-ministerial) mobility. Approximately one-third of the 1949-1959 higher civil servants remained with one ministry throughout their career, and another third began and ended their career in the same ministry, though they transferred to and from other ministries in the interim. This reflects an attitude found also in Japanese business, where moving from one corporation to another is generally considered injurious to career prospects. Administrators expect and are expected to work on a career basis in the government or particular segments of it.

Whether or not low inter-ministerial mobility is desirable is a moot question. Where long service is involved, loyalty to a particular ministry may readily become stronger than loyalty to the public service as a whole. Disputes among ministries over policy issues or appropriations also tend to be more frequent and less amenable to conciliation. Coordination among branches is difficult in any bureaucracy. The problem in Japan does not appear to have been greatly eased by the postwar enlargement of the Prime Minister's authority over other members of the cabinet. Our mobility data tend to show the greatest degree of variation when tabulated by ministry. The statistical measurements developed were consistent with fairly strong compartmentalism, a phenomenon often mentioned in autobiographies by Japanese bureaucrats.

On the other hand, low inter-ministerial mobility has some positive implications. It certainly increases the possibility for bureaucrats to acquire semi-specialized knowledge of a certain area of governmental responsibility. This is one of the principal rebuttals to criticisms of the excessively legal education of Japanese higher civil servants. The traditional concept of elite training has been to acquire at the university level broad knowledge in fields such as law, political science, and economics, which are considered appropriate in developing general managerial and supervisory skills in business or government. Once in the civil service, prospective higher civil servants are encouraged to stay with one ministry, and by the time they become chiefs of section, division and bureau, they are usually acquainted with a variety of administrative functions within that ministry. Our data largely confirm this pattern

164

of personnel administration. While this system may be inferior to that of high functional differentiation, it would certainly be misleading to brand Japanese higher civil servants as "incompetent" or "unqualified" after fifteen or twenty years of experience, simply because their university training was chiefly in law. The relative efficiency of the modern Japanese bureaucracy seems to have been increased by this pattern, although it was initially based less upon a conscious effort to increase functional specialization and skills than upon a traditional preference for low mobility of labor and the factional proclivities of ministries.

SCHOOL CLIQUES

Critics of the bureaucracy contend that school cliques (*gakubatsu*) foster clannishness among higher administrators and discrimination in appointment and promotion. The school cliques thus promote the educational homogeneity of higher civil servants, but the pattern is circular and high educational homogeneity itself provides a basis for school cliques. The validity of this criticism was discussed at some length in Chapter 4. Statistically, the impact of the school cliques on promotion was analyzed in Chapter 5. In addition to higher school cliques and university cliques, considerable evidence also indicated the existence of a Tokyo University Law Faculty clique (*Tōdai Hōgaku bu batsu*) in the higher civil service.

Although it is difficult to elaborate upon the exact nature of the *gakubatsu* system because of its informal structure and workings, some broad characteristics may be noted. The narrow educational base in the recruitment of postwar higher civil servants resembles in some ways the narrow social base of recruitment in the Tokugawa and early Meiji governments. The criteria of selection used by the present government are radically different, but the extent of the resulting group homogeneity is remarkably sim-

165

ilar. It may be said that present higher administrators share as much ingroup feeling as earlier higher administrators. This may well be related to the traditional pattern of thought within the government or even in Japanese culture as a whole.

It is often said that groups are an important unit of analysis in studying social and political relations in Japan, or that groups as a unit of analysis are more relevant to the understanding of Japan than of other nations.[2] Although it is beyond the scope of this study to deal with such a methodological issue, it is clear that our findings indicate the unusual importance of groups in the higher civil service and lend considerable support to such claims for group approaches in studying Japanese society. At the same time, these findings expose the weakness of individualism in the Japanese bureaucracy. While our data do not permit a comprehensive discussion on this question, our analysis of recruitment, transfer, promotion, and retirement casts grave doubts upon the fundamental significance of individuals as against groups. This phenomenon, though it may not be related to what some Japanese historians like to term the "remnants of feudalism," is perhaps to be expected in a nation where democracy has had but a short history.

One must not, however, ignore the positive aspects of this *gakubatsu* system. Above all, the present—especially the post-World War II—method of recruiting prospective higher civil servants is a great improvement over its predecessors. While there is clearly much to be improved in the higher civil service such as the extraordinary concentration of graduates of one university and the enormous stress on seniority and generalists, the present system has made it possible to recruit many of the brightest youths in Japan and has thus contributed enormously to the success of the modern Japanese bureaucracy.

It also seems probable that the *gakubatsu* have tended to pro-

[2] Ishida Takeshi and Irwin Johnson advocate group approaches. See also Robert E. Ward's comment in Lockwood, *op.cit.*, p. 590.

mote stability in the bureaucracy. The political climate in modern Japan has undergone frequent and dramatic changes, and the official governmental philosophy has swung to nearly every point of the ideological spectrum, excluding the extreme left. The greatest shift occurred at the end of World War II, when comprehensive efforts were made under Occupation pressure to democratize all aspects of Japanese life. These changes were anchored in a new constitution and extended into such fields as education, labor, family, land tenure, the economy, and politics. But the higher civil service remained little changed except for minor effects deriving from the purge. This stability is confirmed by this study as well as by others dealing with the Occupation period.[3] By perpetuating the dominance of men with similar educational backgrounds, the *gakubatsu* system promoted the continuity and stability of the administrative machinery as a whole and very possibly its efficiency as well.

Nonetheless, it is questionable whether the *gakubatsu* system is compatible with the basic principles of democracy. Controversy over this issue has long raged in Japan. One of the fundamental barriers to changing the *gakubatsu* is the structure of the Japanese educational system itself. Tokyo University has enjoyed unrivaled prestige in modern Japan, and has been the principal training ground for most Japanese elites. The educational system, especially its primary and secondary levels, was largely reorganized by the Allied Occupation. Nevertheless, Tokyo University clearly remains at the apex of the entire system, supported by ample public funds and the weight of traditional excellence. Bright students in Japan continue to swarm to Tokyo University. It does not seem that this situation will be materially altered in the near future. It would, therefore, be unrealistic to expect that the dominance by Tokyo University graduates in the higher civil service can be eliminated

[3] Baerwald, *op.cit.*, pp. 78-79; Supreme Commander for the Allied Powers, General Headquarters, *op.cit.*, pp. 23-24.

by enacting a civil service reform law, altering the structure of the government, or changing the policy of personnel administration.

STABILITY AND CHANGE

For the 1949-1959 period, the chief characteristics of higher civil servants showed only minor changes. Their social origins, educational backgrounds, and career patterns remained similar, suggesting some underlying forces operating to preserve traditions in the Japanese higher civil service. Certainly, major features of the bureaucracy such as the *gakubatsu* system and the stress upon seniority and generalists showed no decline, but instead manifested symptoms generally associated with the "reverse course." In spite of rapid changes in wartime and postwar Japan, the higher civil service maintained a high degree of continuity and stability.

There were, however, two major exceptions to this general stability. One was the increase in incumbent age; the other the deviative distributions of the 1949 data, especially at the highest level. During the ten years of the survey period, the average age of higher civil servants increased 3.9 years, and the average number of years since university graduation 4.4 years. Although changes of this magnitude may seem trivial to those who are not familiar with the Japanese bureaucracy, this increase in age apparently brought about consequences of considerable importance in the higher civil service, especially in view of the significance of age in Japanese personnel administration. Paralleling the age increase, the average term of office became shorter, and the rate of retirement increased. The average retirement age, while more stable than the average incumbent age, increased slowly but steadily. Although much of the age increase in the 1949-1959 period may be regarded as a natural phenomenon, the lower average age in 1949 was apparently related to special conditions obtaining in that year.

Another major exception was a series of significantly deviative

168

distributions in the 1949 data, especially at the highest level. Similar deviative patterns persisted in the distributions by nearly all major variables. At Level I the proportions of First Higher School graduates, Tokyo University graduates, and law graduates were 25 to 60 percent less than comparable figures in other survey years. Those in 1949 Level I served in fewer ministries, less often in field offices, and more often in nonbureaucratic positions. To a lesser degree, deviative features were also found in lower levels, apparently influenced by the major changes at the highest level. On the other hand, the 1954 and 1959 data showed great similarity in nearly every major distribution.

From these chronological features, it is only a short logical step to the hypothesis that the 1954 and 1959 distributions represent "normalcy," whereas the 1949 distributions were "abnormal" because of the impact of the Allied Occupation. If from the standpoint of theoretical logic in statistics, it is somewhat difficult to attribute the above deviations to the Allied Occupation, it is even more difficult to assume the existence of a contrary condition; that is, that the 1949 distributions represent "normalcy" and the 1954 and 1959 distributions "abnormalcy." First, it is highly unlikely that one would arrive at the kind of distributions found in this study, should the second assumption be correct. Our analysis showed pervasive deviative features for the 1949 data, and high similarity between the 1954 and 1959 data. Although the probability of obtaining this type of distribution and still accepting the second assumption is not nil, it is practically negligible, and certainly less than that favoring the first interpretation. Second, available data for the pre-1949 period give little support to the second assumption. Several studies indicate that the proportion of Tokyo University graduates in that period was very close to our 1954 and 1959 figures but substantially different from our 1949 figures.[4] Also, other studies indicate that a number of civil servants

[4] Inoki, *op.cit.*, p. 296.

at the highest levels were removed from their posts in the immediate postwar period.[5] Therefore, we have reasonable confidence in attributing our 1949 deviative findings to the impact of the Allied Occupation.

ORGANIZATIONAL VARIATIONS

Throughout this study, Japanese higher civil servants revealed fairly large organizational variations, which in many ways exceeded our original expectation. Ministerial variations were generally large regardless of the types of characteristics such as social origins, educational backgrounds, and career patterns. Moreover, these variations did not appear to follow any one underlying pattern. While tabulations by position level tended to result in systematic variations, those by ministry tended to result in fairly irregular variations. The extent of these variations suggests that the ministries are an important variable in our data. The irregularity of these distributions suggests that a variety of secondary factors are operative in producing these ministerial variations.

The complexity of factors involved in the organizational variations of higher civil servants is evident to anyone who examines the career histories of Japanese officials. The origin, reorganization, functional specifications, and transfer patterns of a given ministry inevitably affected the career course of those in that ministry. The civil service examination system and the recruitment policies of various ministries also influenced their careers. These factors sometimes reinforced certain tendencies, but sometimes also detracted from others. It is thus unavoidable that the ministerial distributions of our data display some irregularity.

Among many factors, however, two call for special attention. One was the relative prestige of each ministry; the other, loyalty to a particular ministry. While both concepts, prestige and loyalty,

[5] Baerwald, *op.cit.*, pp. 78-79.

are somewhat nebulous and overlap at many points, it is difficult to deny their force in studying the careers of Japanese higher civil servants. Prestige, as their memoirs make clear, was an important factor for applicants in choosing a ministry, and prestigious ministries in turn tended to recruit those who scored very high in the examinations. Patterns of transfer, term of office, and promotion were also influenced by this factor. Similarly, post-retirement opportunity was related to such prestige rating as shown by the distribution of average retirement ages by ministry.

A closely related, and in many ways supplementary, factor was loyalty to the ministry in which a civil servant began or spent most of his career. In spite of the fact that postwar higher civil servants were highly homogeneous in education, there was a strong tendency to remain with the original ministry. While ministerial prestige influenced ministerial loyalty, such loyalty tended to increase and perpetuate differences among ministries and to foster the development of ministerial cliques (*shōbatsu*). Although this phenomenon is often referred to in memoirs, our data provide some quantitative basis for evaluating ministerial cliques. The magnitude of variations suggests the relative significance of these cliques in the higher civil service. As in the case of the school cliques (*gakubatsu*), we find here another example of the importance of group phenomena in the bureaucracy.

Although it is difficult to summarize these organizational variations by any one measure, an attempt may be made in terms of one of the most important variables, namely age. A two-dimensional scale by incumbent age and retirement age reveals major aspects of the ministerial variations (Figure 14). This summary shows such major features as differences between the core as a whole and the periphery as a whole, relative homogeneity in the core and relative heterogeneity in the periphery, and the gross prestige ranking of the core ministries. Age, as mentioned earlier, is a critical variable in promotion, re-

171

tirement, and many other aspects of personnel administration in the Japanese higher civil service. The fact that the above measure largely summarizes the ministerial variations not only reconfirms the importance of the age variable but also reveals high standardization in the career patterns of higher civil servants and the relative stability of compartmentalism in the Japanese bureaucracy.

However, compartmentalism is to some degree offset by a unifying tendency resulting from high educational homogeneity among the 1949-1959 higher civil servants. Although the degree of dominance by Tokyo University graduates varied from ministry to ministry, it was relatively high in every ministry, especially in comparison with some other bureaucracies or organizations. The influence of the school did not apparently cease at ministerial boundaries. The career patterns of higher civil servants were also reasonably standardized across ministries, and at retirement we find some unifying tendency. Hence, in broad terms, compartmentalism in the bureaucracy may not be as serious a problem as some accounts claim. It does not seem that bureaucratic compartmentalism has been critically hampering governmental operations. It may be disruptive to some degree, but probably not as disruptive as, for instance, factionalism within Japanese political parties.

BUREAUCRACY AND JAPAN

The Japanese are extremely fond of denouncing their own bureaucracy. It is very difficult to find a writer who pays much attention to its positive aspects. Charges of excessive formalism, red tape, inefficiency, conservatism, legalism, and corruption undoubtedly contain some truth. But these criticisms—as with political polemics in most countries—conceal as much as they reveal about the exact role of the Japanese bureaucracy. To contend, for instance, that these deficiencies are peculiar to Japan or that they are paralyzing the nation's administrative machinery is to deny a larger body of evidence showing that this group has been remarkably successful in administering a major nation and in implementing a large number of important social and economic policies.

Nor do these higher civil servants seem as lacking in initiative as is often charged. In Japan, career bureaucrats hold positions normally reserved for political appointees in other countries. They are, for example, heavily involved in such important policy decisions as drafting the annual budgets and formulating long-range economic policies for the nation.[6] Moreover, the effectiveness and efficiency of the higher civil service appear to be independent of political ideology. The bureaucracy has functioned with at least relative success under the Meiji oligarchy, under political parties of the prewar type, under militarist and ultranationalist control, under the Allied Occupation, and now under parliamentary democracy based upon the 1947 Constitution.

It is, however, incorrect to assume from this record that the Japanese bureaucracy has been completely neutral (as the traditional theory of public administration prescribes that it should be) in the face of such radical changes at the highest level of government. Many bureaucrats joined or supported ultranationalist societies.[7] The bureaucracy as a whole participated in the war effort not only in action but also to some extent in spirit. Similarly, since World War II the bureaucracy has not been entirely isolated from the changes in political climate. Important civil service reforms have been undertaken, largely for the purpose of making the bureaucracy more compatible with the principles set forth by the new constitution. The examination system has been modified to reduce the stress on "legalism," and some shift has been made

[6] The Finance Ministry Establishment Law, Article 8; The Economic Counseling Agency (later Economic Planning Agency) Establishment Law, Article 3. The chief of the Budget Bureau in Finance and most councillors to the agency are career civil servants rather than political appointees (professional economists).

[7] Baerwald, *op.cit.*, p. 82.

from a generalist to a more specialist orientation in personnel administration. The *kōtō bunkan* system with its imperial flavor and rigid classification dividing "higher civil servants" (*kōtō bunkan*) from all others is already a thing of the past. The outward signs of hierarchical ordering have been drastically reduced, and the postwar official register, for example, no longer records the ranks or salaries of civil servants.

The idea that a bureaucrat is supposed to be a servant of the public, not a master nor even "the Emperor's aide," now receives far more official support than at any time in the past. The 1947 Constitution included provisions protecting individual rights from official infringement and disestablished the administrative court (*gyōsei saibansho*).[8] That these changes have not been wholly ineffective can be seen from a change in public attitude, which is more openly critical of the bureaucracy than ever before. Whether from conviction or from expediency, the bureaucracy has responded to such changes by making a greater effort to create harmonious relations with the general public and to adjust itself to the new political environment.

Important though these changes may be, the results are perhaps not as great as the legal changes would lead one to believe. Much of the evidence gathered in this study suggests a good deal of continuity and stability in the personnel administration of the higher civil service. While the bureaucracy has probably made considerable progress since the war in public relations, especially in the human rights area, the *kōtō bunkan* system and the practices accompanying it have left important marks on the postwar bureaucracy. Higher civil servants remain nearly as homogeneous as before; and a comparison of the 1949 data with the 1954 and 1959 data indicates a "reverse course" movement against the Occupation reforms. Our analysis of transfer, term of office, promotion,

---

[8] The Constitution, Articles 17, 31-40, and 76.

174

and retirement suggests a very high degree of continuity and stability reinforced by prevailing bureaucratic values and attitudes.

It also seems clear that higher civil servants continue to retain elitist status after retirement. Some of our data suggest, as many Japanese writers have suggested, that the prestige of the higher civil service has declined since World War II, and that opportunities for lucrative and influential post-retirement positions are not quite as substantial as they once were. Nonetheless, not many signs of major change are available. Many retiring civil servants continue to become directors of major corporations, and any reduction of opportunities in the private sector of the economy has been largely offset by expanded opportunities in new public corporations. Even the constitutional changes of 1947, enhancing the power of the Diet at the expense of the executive and making prefectural governorships elective, have not necessarily diminished the chances for retiring civil servants to enter the political arena. Six of the eleven postwar Prime Ministers have been former career civil servants, while other retiring officials have successfully campaigned for election as prefectural governors and Diet members.[9] The advantage of being well known and having acquired certain skills and contacts has proved to be exploitable not only in business but also in the political arena at the highest levels.

Thus, despite some reorientation since World War II, Japanese higher civil servants as a group still enjoy higher social and political status and better prospects for influential post-retirement positions than most of their counterparts in the United States or Great Britain. This is in part a reflection of the fact that in Japan social, economic, and political processes are still strongly colored by a bureaucratic flavor. But this is also in part a reflection of

[9] Shidehara, Yoshida, Ashida, Kishi, Ikeda, and Satō were former career civil servants; Suzuki, Higashikuni, Katayama, Hatoyama, and Ishibashi were not.

the fact that even under the new constitution the higher civil service remained a powerful force within the government.

According to Bendix, a bureaucracy tends to be powerful and to be independent of other organs of the state if it consists of a highly homogeneous group.[10] Although it is difficult to test a thesis of this sort quantitatively, it is noteworthy that it fits the Japanese case reasonably well. Beyond doubt the educational homogeneity of postwar higher civil servants is very high. It also seems that the bureaucracy has tended to stand strong and united against other organs of the state such as the Diet.

There should also be more recognition accorded the fact that the bureaucracy has been critically involved in Japan's social and economic development. In spite of relative instability at the highest levels of government, the bureaucracy apparently has not only discharged its day-to-day tasks in this respect but also implemented long-range policies for the development of the country. It seems probable that higher civil servants will continue to play important roles in Japanese administration and politics. While changes are unavoidable in any bureaucracy, our data suggest an impressive degree of stability for the postwar higher civil service. They also indicate that the informal but powerful school cliques (*gakubatsu*) are likely to retain strong roots in the bureaucracy for years to come. It is further probable that higher civil servants will continue to obtain positions of major importance after leaving the civil service. The continuing process of democratization may be undermining such status and power, but for the moment, the signs of change are too few and too weak to permit much optimism on this score. For years to come Japanese higher civil servants are likely to exert a degree of influence that is impressive by any comparative standards.

[10] Bendix, *op.cit.*, p. 14.

Bibliography

ENGLISH SOURCES

Books

Baerwald, Hans H. *The Purge of Japanese Leaders under the Occupation.* University of California Publication in Political Science, Vol. 8. Berkeley: University of California Press, 1959. 111 pp.

Bendix, Reinhard. *Higher Civil Servants in American Society: A Study of the Social Origins, the Career, and the Power-Position of Higher Federal Administration.* University of Colorado Studies Series in Sociology, No. 1. Boulder, Colorado: University of Colorado Press, 1949. 129 pp.

Berger, Morroe. *Bureaucracy and Society in Modern Egypt: A Study of the Higher Civil Service.* Princeton: Princeton University Press, 1957. 300 pp.

Blalock, Hubert M. *Social Statistics.* New York: McGraw-Hill, 1960. 465 pp.

Burks, Ardath W. *The Government of Japan.* New York: Thomas Y. Crowell, 1961. 269 pp.

Cole, Allan B. *Japanese Society and Politics: The Impact of Social Stratification and Mobility on Politics.* Boston: Department of Government, Boston University, 1956. 158 pp.

Fahs, Charles B. *Government in Japan: Recent Trends in Its Scope and Operation.* New York: Institute of Pacific Relations, 1940. 114 pp.

Hansen, Morris H., William H. Hurwits and William G. Madow. *Sample Survey Methods and Theory*, Vol. 1 (*Methods and Applications*). New York: Wiley, 1953. 638 pp.

177

Heady, Ferrel, and Sybil L. Stokes, comps. *Comparative Public Administration: A Selective Annotated Bibliography*, 2d ed. Ann Arbor, Michigan: Institute of Public Administration, University of Michigan, 1960. 98 pp.

Ho, Ping-ti. *The Ladder of Success in Imperial China: Aspects of Social Mobility, 1368-1911*. New York: Columbia University Press, 1962. 385 pp.

Hoover, Blaine, Manlio F. DeAngelis, Robert S. Hare and W. Pierce MacCoy. *Report of the United States Personnel Advisory Mission to Japan*, Vol. 1, Submitted to the Supreme Commander for the Allied Powers. Unpublished, 1947.

Ike, Nobutaka. *Japanese Politics: An Introductory Survey*. New York: Knopf, 1957. 300 pp.

Kawai, Kazuo. *Japan's American Interlude*. Chicago: University of Chicago Press, 1960. 277 pp.

Kelsall, R. K. *Higher Civil Servants in Britain from 1870 to the Present Day*. London: Routledge and Kegan Paul, 1955. 233 pp.

Kilpatrick, Franklin P., Milton C. Cummings, Jr., and M. Kent Jennings. *The Image of the Federal Service*. Washington, D.C.: Brookings Institution, 1964. 301 pp.

————. *Source Book of a Study of Occupational Values and the Image of the Federal Service*. Washington, D.C.: Brookings Institution, 1964. 681 pp.

LaPalombara, Joseph, ed. *Bureaucracy and Political Development*. Princeton: Princeton University Press, 1963. 487 pp.

Linebarger, Paul M. A., Djang Chu, and Ardath Burks. *Far Eastern Governments and Politics: China and Japan*, 2d ed. Princeton: Van Nostrand, 1956. 643 pp.

McNelly, Theodore. *Contemporary Government of Japan*. Boston: Houghton Mifflin, 1963. 228 pp.

Maki, John M. *Government and Politics in Japan*. New York: Praeger, 1962. 275 pp.

178

Matthews, Donald R. *The Social Background of Political Decision-Makers*. Doubleday Short Studies in Political Science. Garden City, N.Y.: Doubleday, 1954. 71 pp.

Menzel, Johanna M., ed. *The Chinese Civil Service: Career Open to Talent?* Problems in Asian Civilization. Boston: D. C. Heath, 1963. 110 pp.

Montgomery, John D. *Forced to Be Free: The Artificial Revolution in Germany and Japan*. Chicago: University of Chicago Press, 1957. 209 pp.

————. *The Purge in Occupied Japan: A Study in the Use of Civilian Agencies under Military Government*. Technical Memorandum ORO-T-48 (FEC). Chevy Chase, Maryland: Operations Research Office, Johns Hopkins University Press, 1954. 381 pp.

Morstein Marx, Fritz, ed. *Elements of Public Administration*, 2d ed. Englewood Cliffs, N.J.: Prentice-Hall, 1959. 572 pp.

Munakata, Peter Francis. *The Application of Western Sociological Theory to the Analysis of Bureaucratic Structure in Japan: A Pilot Study and Its Interpretation*. Unpublished Ph.D. Dissertation, Fordham University, 1956.

Quigley, Harold S. *Japanese Government and Politics: An Introductory Study*. New York: Century, 1932. 442 pp.

Quigley, Harold S., and John E. Turner. *The New Japan: Government and Politics*. Minneapolis: University of Minnesota Press, 1956. 456 pp.

Reischauer, Robert K. *Japan: Government—Politics*. New York: Nelson, 1939. 221 pp.

Scalapino, Robert A., and Junnosuke Masumi. *Parties and Politics in Contemporary Japan*. Berkeley: University of California Press, 1962. 190 pp.

Silberman, Bernard S. *Ministers of Modernization: Elite Mobility in the Meiji Restoration 1868-1873*. Tucson, Arizona: University of Arizona Press, 1964. 135 pp.

Slesinger, Jonathan Avery. *Personnel Adaptations in the Federal Junior Management Assistant Program.* Michigan Governmental Studies No. 41. Ann Arbor, Mich.: Institute of Public Administration, University of Michigan, 1961. 146 pp.

Supreme Commander for the Allied Powers, Government Section. *Political Reorientation of Japan, September 1945 to September 1948, Report.* Washington, D.C.: U.S. Government Printing Office, 1949. 1300 pp. in 2 vols.

Supreme Commander for the Allied Powers, General Headquarters. *History of Nonmilitary Activities of the Occupation of Japan, 1945-1951,* Vol. V, Part 6, Reorganization of Civil Service (1945-1951). Unpublished, 1951. 207 pp.

Ward, Robert E., and Roy C. Macridis, eds. *Modern Political Systems: Asia.* Englewood Cliffs, N.J.: Prentice-Hall, 1963. 482 pp.

Ward, Robert E., and Dankwart A. Rustow, eds. *Political Modernization in Japan and Turkey.* Princeton: Princeton University Press, 1964. 502 pp.

Warner, W. Lloyd, Paul P. Van Riper, Norman H. Martin and Orvis F. Collins. *The American Federal Executive: A Study of the Social and Personal Characteristics of the Civilian and Military Leaders of the United States Federal Government.* New Haven: Yale University Press, 1963. 405 pp.

White, Leonard D., ed. *The Civil Service in the Modern State: A Collection of Documents Published under the Auspices of the International Congress of the Administrative Services.* Chicago: University of Chicago Press, 1930. 563 pp.

Yanaga, Chitoshi. *Japanese People and Politics.* New York: Wiley, 1956. 408 pp.

Articles

Abegglen, James C., and Hiroshi Mannari. "Leaders of Modern Japan: Social Origins and Mobility," *Economic Development*

180

and Cultural Change, Vol. 9, No. 2, Part 2 (October 1960), pp. 109-134.

Adachi, Tadao. "The Administrative Group and Its Problems: The CSS Blueprint of a Reform in the Civil Service," *Kwansai Gakuin University Annual Studies,* Vol. 7 (1959), pp. 285-299.

————. "The Patterns of Administration in the Public Service: An Interpretation of the Public Service in Japan," *Kwansai Gakuin Law Review,* Annual Report, Vol. 1 (1962), pp. 1-20.

Brady, James B. "Japanese Administrative Behavior and the 'Sala' Model," *Philippine Journal of Public Administration,* Vol. 8, No. 4 (October 1964), pp. 314-324.

Braibanti, Ralph J. "The Role of Administration in the Occupation of Japan," *Annals of the American Academy of Political and Social Science,* Vol. 207 (January 1950), pp. 154-163.

Burks, Ardath W. "A Note on the Emerging Administrative Structure of the Post-Treaty Japanese National Government," *Occasional Papers,* Center for Japanese Studies, No. 3 (1952), pp. 47-58. Ann Arbor, Mich.: University of Michigan Press, 1952.

Esman, Milton J. "Japanese Administration: A Comparative View," *Public Administration Review,* Vol. 7, No. 2 (Spring 1947), pp. 100-112.

MacDonald, Hugh H., and Milton J. Esman. "The Japanese Civil Service," *Public Personnel Review,* Vol. 7, No. 4 (October 1946), pp. 213-224.

Maki, John M. "Prime Minister's Office and Executive Power in Japan," *Far Eastern Survey,* Vol. 24, No. 4 (May 1955), pp. 71-75.

————. "Role of the Bureaucracy in Japan," *Pacific Affairs,* Vol. 20, No. 4 (December 1947), pp. 391-406.

Mannari, Hiroshi. "A Study of the Social Origins and the Career Patterns of the Higher Civil Servants in the Japanese Foreign Service," *Kwansai Gakuin University Annual Studies,* Vol. 6 (1958), pp. 77-102.

Roser, Foster B. "Establishing a Modern Merit System in Japan," *Public Personnel Review*, Vol. 11, No. 4 (October 1950), pp. 199-206.

Shirven, Maynard N., and Joseph L. Speicher. "Examination of Japan's Upper Bureaucracy," *Personnel Administration*, Vol. 14, No. 4 (July 1951), pp. 48-57.

Tsuji, Kiyoaki. "The Cabinet, Administrative Organization, and the Bureaucracy," *Annals of the American Academy of Political and Social Science*, Vol. 308 (November 1956), pp. 10-17.

————. "Public Administration in Japan," S. S. Hsueh, ed., *Public Administration in South and South Asia*. Brussels: International Institute of Administrative Sciences, 1962, pp. 51-63.

JAPANESE SOURCES

Books

Adachi, Tadao. *Kindai kanryōsei to shokkaisei* (Modern Bureaucracy and Position Classification Systems). Tokyo: Gakuyō Shobō, 1952. 262 pp.

Fukuchi, Shigetaka. *Shizoku to samurai ishiki: Kindai Nihon o okoseru mono horobosu mono* (The Samurai Class and Samurai Class Consciousness: A Factor Building and Destroying Modern Japan). Tokyo: Shunjūsha, 1956. 356 pp.

Imai, Kazuo. *Kanryō* (Bureaucrats). Tokyo: Yomiuri Shimbunsha, 1953. 335 pp.

Kainō, Michitaka et al., eds. *Nihon shihonshugi kōza* (Lectures on Japanese Capitalism), Vol. 3 (Politics and Economics in Post-War Japan). Tokyo: Iwanami Shoten, 1953. 415 pp.

Kanryōseido Kenkyūkai, comp. *Kanryō* (Bureaucrats). Kyōto: Sanichi Shobō, 1959. 246 pp.

Kawanaka, Nikō. *Gendai no kanryōsei: Kōmuin no kanri taisei* (The Contemporary Bureaucracy: Systems of Personnel Administration). Tokyo: Chūō University Press, 1962. 166 pp.

182

Maeda, Tamon, and Takagi Yasaka, eds. *Nitobe hakushi tsuioku shū* (An Anthology of Articles and Speeches Commemorating Dr. Nitobe). Tokyo: Ko Nitobe Hakushi Kinen Jigyō Iinkai, 1936. 577 pp.

Mainichi Shimbunsha, comp. *Kanryō Nippon* (Bureaucratic Japan). Tokyo: Mainichi Shimbunsha, 1956. 279 pp.

Matsumoto, Seichō. *Gendai kanryō ron* (On Contemporary Bureaucrats). Tokyo: Bungei Shunjūsha, 1963. 273 pp.

Miyake, Tarō. *Jinjikanri to kōmuin* (Personnel Administration and Public Servants). Tokyo: Ryōsho Fukyūkai, 1949. 240 pp.

Naiseimondai Kenkyūkai, comp. *Kanryō no keifu* (Genealogies of Bureaucrats). Tokyo: Kōbunsha, 1954. 223 pp.

Nihon Hyōronsha, comp. *Nihon no hōgaku: Kaiko to tembō* (Japanese Jurisprudence: Recollection and Prospect). Tokyo: Nihon Hyōronsha, 1950. 402 pp.

Okabe, Shirō. *Kōmuinseido no kenkyū* (A Study of the Public Service). Tokyo: Yūshindō, 1955. 352 pp.

Tanaka, Sōgorō. *Nihon kanryō seijishi* (A Political History of the Japanese Bureaucracy). Tokyo: Kawade Shobō, 1954. 254 pp.

Tsuji, Kiyoaki. *Nihon kanryōsei no kenkyū* (A Study of the Japanese Bureaucracy). Tokyo: Kōbundō, 1952. 292 pp.

Usui, Yoshimi, ed. *Gendai kyōyō zenshū* (A Collection of Works on the Contemporary Culture), Vol. 21 (Bureaucrats, Political Parties and Pressure Groups). Tokyo: Chikuma Shobō, 1960. 399 pp.

Yoshimura, Tadashi. *Gendai seiji ni okeru kanryō no chii* (The Position of Bureaucrats in Contemporary Politics). Tokyo: Maeno Shoten, 1950. 525 pp.

Articles

Asō, Makoto. "Meijiki ni okeru kōtō kyōiku shokikan no erīto keisei kinō ni kansuru kenkyū" (A Study of the Function of

Higher Education in Producing Elites in the Meiji Era), *Kyōikugaku kenkyū*, Vol. 30, No. 2 (May 1963), pp. 109-124.

―――. Meiji zenki (yōranki) kōtō kyōiku no shokeitai to sono erīto keisei kōka ni kansuru kenkyū" (A Study of the Forms of Higher Education and Its Effects in Producing Elites in the Early Meiji Period), *Nihon Ikueikai kenkyū kiyō*, Vol. 1 (May 1963), Appendix I, pp. 69-96.

Tsuji, Kiyoaki. "Kōmuinseido no kaikaku" (A Reform of the Public Service System), *Kōhō Kenkyū*, No. 7 (1952), pp. 42-57.

Japanese Government Publications

Mombu Daijin Kambō Hishoka (Minister of Education, Secretariat, Secretary Section), comp. *Dai Nihon Teikoku Mombu Shō nempō* (The Annual Report of the Ministry of Education, the Great Japanese Empire), 1873+.

Naikaku Kambō (Cabinet, Secretariat), comp. *Naikaku seido shichijūnenshi* (Seventy-Year History of the Cabinet System). Tokyo: Ōkurashō Insatsu Kyoku (Ministry of Finance, Printing Bureau), 1955. 690 pp.

Nōrin Daijin Kambō Hishoka (Minister of Agriculture and Forestry, Secretariat, Secretary Section), comp. *Jinji gyōsei no kiso genri* (Fundamental Principles of Personnel Administration) Tokyo: Nōrin Daijin Kambō Bunshoka (Minister of Agriculture and Forestry, Secretariat, Archives Section), 1949. 258 pp.

Ōkura Shō Insatsu Kyoku (Ministry of Finance, Printing Bureau), comp. *Hōrei zensho* (Compendium of Laws and Ordinances). Tokyo: Ōkura Shō Insatsu Kyoku (Ministry of Finance, Printing Bureau), 1885+.

―――. *Shokuin roku* (Official Register). Tokyo: Ōkura Shō Insatsu Kyoku (Ministry of Finance, Printing Bureau), 1947+.

Sōri Fu Kambō Kansa Ka (Prime Minister's Office, Secretariat, Review Section), comp. *Kōshoku tsuihō ni kansuru oboegaki gaitōsha meibo* (A List of Purged Individuals). Tokyo: Hibiya Seikeikai, 1949.

Sōri Fu Tōkei Kyoku (Prime Minister's Office, Statistics Bureau), comp. *Nihon tōkei nenkan* (Japan Statistical Yearbook). Tokyo: Nihon Tōkei Kyōkai, 1882-1941, 1949+.

————. *Kokusei chōsa hōkoku* (Population Census of Japan). Tokyo: Ōkura Shō Insatsu Kyoku (Ministry of Finance, Printing Bureau), 1928+.

Sōri Fu Yoron Chōsajo (Prime Minister's Office, Public Opinion Institute), comp. (*Jinji gyōsei ni kansuru yoron chōsa* (A Public Opinion Survey on Personnel Administration). Tokyo: Sōri Fu Yoron Chōsajo (Prime Minister's Office, Institute of Public Opinion), 1951. 20 pp.

Biographical Dictionaries and Reference Materials

Hirose, Hiroshi et al., comps. *Shokugyō betsu taishū jinji roku* (Who's Who by Occupation). Tokyo: Himitsu Tanteisha, 1925+.

Jinji Kōshinjo, comp. *Jinji kōshin roku* (Who's Who). Tokyo: Jinji Kōshinjo, 1903+.

————. *Zen Nihon shinshi roku* (Who's Who in All Japan). Tokyo: Jinji Kōshinjo, 1950+.

Nihon Kankai Jōhōsha, comp. *Nihon kankai meikan* (Who's Who in the Japanese Government). Tokyo: Nihon Kankai Jōhōsha, 1936+.

Nihon Shinshi Roku Hensan Jimusho, comp. *Nihon shinshi roku* (Who's Who in Japan). Tokyo: Kōjunsha, 1889+.

Tōdai Sotsugyōsei Meibo Hensan Iinkai (The Committee for Compiling a Directory of Tokyo University Graduates), comp. *Tōdai jinmei roku: Kanchō hen* (Directory of Tokyo University Graduates: Government and Public Corporation Section). Tokyo: Tōdai Sotsugyōsei Meibo Hensan Iinkai, 1960 and 1962.

185

BIBLIOGRAPHY

Ichikō Dōsōkai (The First Higher School Alumni Association), comp. *Kaiin meibo* (Directory). Tokyo: Ichikō Dōsōkai, 1939.

Nikō Shōshisha (The Second Higher School Shōshisha), comp. *Nikō meibo* (Second Higher School Directory). Tokyo: Nikō Shōshisha, 1956.

Sankō Dōsōkai (The Third Higher School Alumni Association), comp. *Kaiin meibo* (Directory) [Kyōto?]: Sankō Dōsōkai, 1962.

Daiyon Kōtō Gakkō Dōsōkai (The Fourth Higher School Alumni Association), comp. *Kaiin meibo* (Directory). Tokyo: Daiyon Kōtō Gakkō Dōsōkai, 1955.

Gōkō Dōsōkai (The Fifth Higher School Alumni Association), comp. *Kaiin meibo* (Directory). Kumamoto: Gōkō Dōsōkai, 1943, 1953, and 1960.

Dairoku Kōtō Gakkō Dōsōkai (The Sixth Higher School Alumni Association), comp. *Kaiin meibo* (Directory). Okayama: Rokkō Dōsōkai, 1962.

Shichikō Dōsōkai (The Seventh Higher School Alumni Association), comp. *Kaiin meibo* (Directory). Kagoshima: Shichikō Dōsōkai, 1962.

Hachikō Sōritsu Gojūnen Kinen Jigyō Jikkō Iinkai (The Executive Committee for the Celebration of the Fiftieth Anniversary of the Eighth Higher School), comp. *Daihachi Kōtō Gakkō Dōsōkai kaiin meibo* (Eighth Higher School Alumni Directory). Nagoya: Hachikō Sōritsu Gojūnen Kinen Jigyō Jikkō Iinkai, 1958.

Daikō Kurabu (Ōsaka Higher School Club), comp. *Ōsaka Kōtō Gakkō Dōsōkai kaiin meibo* (Ōsaka Higher School Alumni Directory). Ōsaka: Daikō Kurabu, 1959.

Kanritsu Hirosaki Kōtō Gakkō Dōsōkai (The State Operated Hirosaki Higher School Alumni Association), comp. *Kaiin meibo* (Directory). Hirosaki: Kanritsu Hirosaki Kōtō Gakkō Dōsōkai, 1960.

186

Kyūsei Kōchi Kōtō Gakkō Dōsōkai (The Former Kōchi Higher School Alumni Association), comp. *Kaiin meibo* (Directory). Kōchi: Kyūsei Kōchi Kōtō Gakkō Dōsōkai, 1962.

Kyūsei Matsue Kōtō Gakkō Dōsōkai (The Former Matsue Higher School Alumni Association), comp. *Dōsōkaiin meibo* (Alumni Directory). Matsue: Kyūsei Matsue Kōtō Gakkō Dōsōkai, 1963.

Seiryōkai (Fukuoka Higher School Seiryōkai), comp. *Kaiin meibo* (Directory). Fukuoka: Seiryōkai Hombu, 1962.

Urawa Kōtō Gakkō Dōsōkai (Urawa Higher School Alumni Association), comp. *Kaiin meibo* (Directory). Urawa: Urawa Kōtō Gakkō Dōsōkai, 1942.

Ishizaki Ryū. *Jinji In Kisoku oyobi kankei hōki* (National Personnel Authority Ordinances and Related Laws). Tokyo: Ishizaki Shoten, 1949+.

Jiji Tsūshinsha, comp. *Jiji nenkan* (Yearbook of Current Events). Tokyo: Jiji Tsūshinsha, 1947+.

Kindai Nihon Kyōiku Seido Shiryō Hensankai, comp. *Kindai Nihon kyōiku seido shiryō* (Historical Materials on the Modern Japanese Education System). Tokyo: Dai Nihon Yūbenkai Kōdansha. 1956+.

Tōkyō Daigaku Shakaikagaku Kenkyūjo (Tokyo University, Institute for Social Research), comp. *Kanryōsei bunken moku roku* (A Bibliography on Bureaucracy). Seiji jittai kenkyū shiryō, No. 2. Tokyo: Tōkyō Daigaku Shakaikagaku Kenkyūjo, 1956.

Wagatsuma, Sakae and Miyazawa Toshiyoshi, comps. *Roppō zensho* (Compendium of the Six Codes). Tokyo: Yūhikaku, 1948+.

Index*

* A "t" following page number means the reference is to a table.

189

bureaucracy, 3, 4; reform in, 5; other studies of, 6; independence, 17; reorganization, 18, 98; British, 67n, 71, 162; functional specialization, 83-84; development, 105; history, 105; inefficiency, 121; efficiency, 122; morale, 122; functional differentiation, 122; promotion in, 122; stability, 167, 168-70, 174-75; change, 168-70; neutrality, 173; continuity, 174-75; power, 176

bureaucracy and Japan, 172-76

bureaucrats "as the Emperor's aides," 5, 174; as "servants of the people," 5, 174

bushi, 54. *See also* samurai

business, 155, 156, 157

Cabinet (*Naikaku*), 4, 11, 12, 111; ministries (*shō*), 10; minister (*daijin*), 11, 47, 158; Secretariat (*Naikaku Kambō*), 12, 24n; Legislation Bureau, 120

Cambridge University, 71, 162

career appointments, 11

career officials, 4, 5, 15, 17

career patterns, 92; standardization in, 163-65, 172

career service, 92

careers, political, 5; nonbureaucratic, 92-97

China, rural bureaucratic elite in, 37

chokunin, 26fig, 27. *See also* higher civil servants

Choshū, 27, 28

chronological changes, 92, 97, 100, 125, 168; in age distribution, 43; in terms of office, 116, 117, 118; in retirement practices, 149

Chūō University, 68, 69t, 70n

cities, 38

class status, 54-56; legal distinctions, 54

colleges: commercial, agricultural, technical, 70; in United States, 78

committees, government, 155

commoners, 54, 55

communications corporations, 156

Communications Ministry, 63

compartmentalism, 164, 172

conservatism, 138, 172

Constitution (1947), 4, 5, 10, 11n, 167, 173, 174n

Constitutional Research Council (*Kempō Chōsa Kai*), 12

control, 28n

Construction Bureau, 99, 105

Construction Ministry (*Kensetsu Shō*), 9, 13, 24

consultants (*san'yo*), 17. *See also* specialists

core, 10, 11, 15-23, 38, 95, 113

corporation officers, 47

correlation, 127n, 133, 134fig, 135-39, 144

corruption, 172

Council on Social Security System, 9

councillors (*shingi kan*), 17, 82

Court Establishment Law, 144n

court nobles (*kuge*), 54

critics, 93, 95

death, 156

Defense Agency, 110

Defense as branch of National Public Service, 25fig

demotion, 128

Diet, 4, 6, 8, 9, 176; members, 47, 158; employees, 155

diplomatic corps, 118

Diplomatic Public Service Law, 143n

diplomatic relations, 15

diplomats, 10-11, 19, 20; recruitment of, 95-96. *See also* ambassadors, ministers

divisions (*bu*), 14, 15, 18, 43, 44; chiefs, 14, 19; assistant chiefs, 14, 19

economics faculty, 79t, 80

economics in higher civil service examinations, 68

Economic Counseling Agency, 98, 98n; Establishment Law, 173n